COMMON CORE

MATH

Activities that Captivate, Motivate & Reinforce

Grade 5

by Marjorie Frank

Incentive Publications, Inc.
Nashville, Tennessee

Illustrated by Kathleen Bullock
Cover by Penny Laporte
Edited by Joy MacKenzie

ISBN 978-0-86530-743-8

1 2 3 4 5 6 7 8 9 10   15   14   13   12

Printed by Sheridan Books, Inc., Chelsea, Michigan • October 2012
www.incentivepublications.com

CONTENTS

Number and Operations in Base Ten

Number and Operations—Fractions

Measurement and Data

Geometry

Assessment & Answer Keys

Great Support for Common Core Standards!

Invite your students to join in on mysteries and adventures with colorful characters! They will delight in the high-appeal topics and engaging visuals. They can

   . . . follow the plot of record-setting bathtub racers;

   . . . solve real-life problems about elephant lifting and cricket spitting;

   . . . check out a torch-throwing practice or milkshake-gulping contest;

   . . . imagine what it would be like to spend two years sitting in a tree or an hour sitting in a bathtub with 35 rattlesnakes;

   . . . meet some totally-tattooed characters;

   . . . juggle data on extreme mosquito-swatting, shoe shining, and egg balancing;

   . . . adapt a recipe to feed twelve hungry weightlifters,

   . . . help a skater leap and swerve through an obstacle course;

   . . . figure out how far someone can walk on hot plates (in bare feet);

   . . . and tackle many other delightful tasks.

Record-setter, Willy Wobble.

And while they engage in these ventures, they will be moving toward competence with critical math skills, processes, and standards that they need for success in the real world.

How to Use this Book

- The pages are tools to support your teaching of the concepts, processes, and skills outlined in the Common Core State Standards. This is not a curriculum; it is a collection of engaging experiences for you to use as you do math with your children or students.

- Use any given page to introduce, explain, teach, practice, extend, assess, provide independent work, start a discussion about, or get students collaborating on a skill or concept.

- Use any page in a large group or small group setting to deepen understandings and expand knowledge or skill. Pages are not intended solely for independent work. Do them together, or always review and discuss the work together.

- Each activity is focused on a particular standard, but most make use of or can be expanded to strengthen other standards as well.

- The book is organized according to the Common Core math domains. Use the tables on pages 9–16 and the label at the bottom corner of each activity page to identify the standard category supported by each page.

- Use the labels on the Contents pages to see specific standards/skills for each page.

- For further mastery of Common Core State Standards, use the suggestions on the next page (page 8).

About Common Core Math Standards

The Common Core State Math Standards seek to expand conceptual understanding of the key ideas of math while they strengthen foundational skills, operations, and principles. They identify what students should know, understand, and be able to do— with an emphasis on explaining principles and applying them to a wide range of situations. To best help students gain and master these robust standards for math . . .

1. Know the standards well. Keep them in front of you. Understand for yourself the big picture of what the standards seek to do. (See www.corestandards.org.)

2. Work to apply, expand, and deepen student skills. With activities in this book (or any learning activities), plan to include

    . . . interaction with peers in pairs, small groups, and large groups

    . . . plenty of discussion, integration, and hands-on work with math concepts

    . . . emphasis on questioning, analyzing, modeling math situations, explaining what you are doing and thinking, using tools effectively, and applying to real world problems

    . . . lots of observation, meaningful feedback, follow-up, and reflection

3. Ask questions that advance reasoning, application, and real-life connection:

- *What, exactly, IS the problem?*
- *Can you solve this another way?*
- *Does this make sense? (Why or why not?)*
- *Can you state the problem in a different way?*
- *What information is needed to solve this problem?*
- *What information in the problem is not needed?*
- *What operations do you need to use?*
- *If we change ____, what will happen to ____?*
- *What tools do you need to solve this?*
- *Can you draw your problem-solving process?*
- *What did you learn from solving this problem?*
- *When could you use this? Where could you use this?*
- *Now that you know how to ____, where can you use this?*

- *How did you arrive at your answer?*
- *How can you show that your answer is right?*
- *Where else have you seen a problem like this?*
- *What does this ask you to do?*
- *What led you to this conclusion?*
- *How could we figure this out?*
- *What was the first step you took?*
- *What information is missing?*
- *How could you make a model of this?*
- *How could you draw your solution?*
- *How do you know this is right?*
- *What patterns do you notice?*
- *Where have you seen this in real life?*
- *What does this remind you of?*
- *Could there be another answer?*
- *If this is true, what else might be true?*
- *How can you explain your answer?*
- *Could you ask that question differently?*
- *What will you do next?*

Standards for Mathematical Practice

St. #	Standard	Pages in This Book
1	Make sense of problems and persevere in solving them.	18–18, 30–58, 60–88, 90–106, 108–126
2	Reason abstractly and quantitatively.	18–18, 30–58, 60–88, 90–106, 108–126
3	Construct viable arguments and critique the reasoning of others.	35, 36, 41, 52, 55, 64, 65, 75, 76, 77, 84, 85, 86, 87, 88, 96–106
4	Model with mathematics.	18–24, 37–40, 60–88, 93–106, 108–126
5	Use appropriate tools strategically.	73, 74, 93–120
6	Attend to precision.	18–28, 30–58, 60–88, 90–106, 108–126
7	Look for and make use of structure.	18–28, 33–40, 73–81, 108–126
8	Look for and express regularity in repeated reasoning.	18–28, 33–36, 93–120

Grade 5 Common Core State Standards for Mathematical Content

5.OA   Operations and Algebraic Thinking

St. #	Standard	Pages in This Book
	Write and interpret numerical expressions.	
1	Use parentheses, brackets, or braces in numerical expressions, and evaluate expressions with these symbols.	18, 19, 20, 21
2	Write simple expressions that record calculations with numbers, and interpret numerical expressions without evaluating them. *For example, express the calculation "add 8 and 7, then multiply by 2" as 2 × (8 + 7). Recognize that 3 × (18932 + 921) is three times as large as 18932 + 921, without having to calculate the indicated sum or product.*	22, 23, 24
	Generate and analyze patterns.	
3	Generate two numerical patterns using two given rules. Identify apparent relationships between corresponding terms. Form ordered pairs consisting of corresponding terms from the two patterns, and graph the ordered pairs on a coordinate plane. *For example, given the rule "Add 3" and the starting number 0, and given the rule "Add 6" and the starting number 0, generate terms in the resulting sequences, and observe that the terms in one sequence are twice the corresponding terms in the other sequence. Explain informally why this is so.*	25, 26, 27, 28

Grade 5 Common Core State Standards for Mathematical Content

5.NBT Number and Operations in Base Ten

St. #	Standard	Pages in This Book
	Understand the place value system.	
1	Recognize that in a multi-digit whole number, a digit in one place represents ten times what it represents in the place to its right and 1/10 of what it represents in the place to its left.	30, 31, 32
2	Explain patterns in the number of zeros of the product when multiplying a number by powers of 10, and explain patterns in the placement of the decimal point when a decimal is multiplied or divided by a power of 10. Use whole-number exponents to denote powers of 10.	33, 34, 35, 36
3	Read, write, and compare decimals to thousandths.	
3a	Read and write decimals to thousandths using base-ten numerals, number names, and expanded form, e.g., $347.392 = 3 \times 100 + 4 \times 10 + 7 \times 1 + 3 \times (1/10) + 9 \times (1/100) + 2 \times (1/1000)$.	37, 38, 39, 40
3b	Compare two decimals to thousandths based on meanings of the digits in each place, using >, =, and < symbols to record the results of comparisons.	41, 42, 43
4	Use place value understanding to round decimals to any place.	44, 45, 46
	Perform operations with multi-digit whole numbers and with decimals to hundredths.	
5	Fluently multiply multi-digit whole numbers using the standard algorithm.	47, 48, 49, 50, 51
6	Find whole-number quotients of whole numbers with up to four-digit dividends and two-digit divisors, using strategies based on place value, the properties of operations, and/or the relationship between multiplication and division. Illustrate and explain the calculation by using equations, rectangular arrays, and/or area models.	50, 51, 52, 53, 54
7	Add, subtract, multiply, and divide decimals to hundredths, using concrete models or drawings and strategies based on place value, properties of operations, and/or the relationship between addition and subtraction; relate the strategy to a written method and explain the reasoning used.	55, 56, 57, 58

11

Grade 5 Common Core State Standards for Mathematical Content

5.NBT   Number and Operations—Fractions

St. #	Standard	Pages in This Book
	Use equivalent fractions as a strategy to add and subtract fractions.	
1	Add and subtract fractions with unlike denominators (including mixed numbers) by replacing given fractions with equivalent fractions in such a way as to produce an equivalent sum or difference of fractions with like denominators. *For example, 2/3 + 5/4 = 8/12 + 15/12 = 23/12. (In general, a/b + c/d = (ad + bc)/bd.)*	60, 61, 62, 63, 64, 65
2	Solve word problems involving addition and subtraction of fractions referring to the same whole, including cases of unlike denominators, e.g., by using visual fraction models or equations to represent the problem. Use benchmark fractions and number sense of fractions to estimate mentally and assess the reasonableness of answers. *For example, recognize an incorrect result 2/5 + 1/2 = 3/7, by observing that 3/7 < 1/2.*	63, 64, 65
	Apply and extend previous understandings of multiplication and division to multiply and divide fractions.	
3	Interpret a fraction as division of the numerator by the denominator (a/b = a ÷ b). Solve word problems involving division of whole numbers leading to answers in the form of fractions or mixed numbers, e.g., by using visual fraction models or equations to represent the problem. *For example, interpret 3/4 as the result of dividing 3 by 4, noting that 3/4 multiplied by 4 equals 3, and that when 3 wholes are shared equally among 4 people each person has a share of size 3/4. If 9 people want to share a 50-pound sack of rice equally by weight, how many pounds of rice should each person get? Between what two whole numbers does your answer lie?*	66, 67, 68
4	Apply and extend previous understandings of multiplication to multiply a fraction or whole number by a fraction.	
4a	Interpret the product (a/b) × q as a parts of a partition of q into b equal parts; equivalently, as the result of a sequence of operations a × q ÷ b. *For example, use a visual fraction model to show (2/3) × 4 = 8/3, and create a story context for this equation. Do the same with (2/3) × (4/5) = 8/15. (In general, (a/b) × (c/d) = ac/bd.)*	69, 70, 71, 72, 73, 74
4b	Find the area of a rectangle with fractional side lengths by tiling it with unit squares of the appropriate unit fraction side lengths, and show that the area is the same as would be found by multiplying the side lengths. Multiply fractional side lengths to find areas of rectangles, and represent fraction products as rectangular areas.	73, 74

Grade 5 Common Core State Standards for Mathematical Content

5.NBT Number and Operations—Fractions, continued

St. #	Standard	Pages in This Book
5	Interpret multiplication as scaling (resizing), by:	
5a	Comparing the size of a product to the size of one factor on the basis of the size of the other factor, without performing the indicated multiplication.	75
5b	Explaining why multiplying a given number by a fraction greater than 1 results in a product greater than the given number (recognizing multiplication by whole numbers greater than 1 as a familiar case); explaining why multiplying a given number by a fraction less than 1 results in a product smaller than the given number; and relating the principle of fraction equivalence $a/b = (n \times a)/(n \times b)$ to the effect of multiplying a/b by 1.	76, 77
6	Solve real world problems involving multiplication of fractions and mixed numbers, e.g., by using visual fraction models or equations to represent the problem.	79, 80, 81
7	**Apply and extend previous understandings of division to divide unit fractions by whole numbers and whole numbers by unit fractions.**	
7a	Interpret division of a unit fraction by a non-zero whole number, and compute such quotients. *For example, create a story context for (1/3) ÷ 4, and use a visual fraction model to show the quotient. Use the relationship between multiplication and division to explain that (1/3) ÷ 4 = 1/12 because (1/12) × 4 = 1/3.*	82, 83, 86, 87, 88
7b	Interpret division of a whole number by a unit fraction, and compute such quotients. *For example, create a story context for 4 ÷ (1/5), and use a visual fraction model to show the quotient. Use the relationship between multiplication and division to explain that 4 ÷ (1/5) = 20 because 20 × (1/5) = 4.*	84, 85, 86, 87, 88
7c	Solve real world problems involving division of unit fractions by non-zero whole numbers and division of whole numbers by unit fractions, e.g., by using visual fraction models and equations to represent the problem. *For example, how much chocolate will each person get if 3 people share 1/2 lb of chocolate equally? How many 1/3-cup servings are in 2 cups of raisins?*	86, 87, 88

Grade 5 Common Core State Standards for Mathematical Content

5.MD   Measurement and Data

St. #	Standard	Pages in This Book
Convert like measurement units within a given measurement system.		
1	Convert among different-sized standard measurement units within a given measurement system (e.g., convert 5 cm to 0.05 m), and use these conversions in solving multi-step, real world problems.	90, 91, 92
Represent and interpret data.		
2	Make a line plot to display a data set of measurements in fractions of a unit (1/2, 1/4, 1/8). Use operations on fractions for this grade to solve problems involving information presented in line plots. *For example, given different measurements of liquid in identical beakers, find the amount of liquid each beaker would contain if the total amount in all the beakers were redistributed equally.*	93, 94, 95, 96, 97, 98, 99
Geometric measurement: understand concepts of volume and relate volume to multiplication and to addition.		
3	Recognize volume as an attribute of solid figures and understand concepts of volume measurement.	
3a	A cube with side length 1 unit, called a "unit cube," is said to have "one cubic unit" of volume, and can be used to measure volume.	100, 101
3b	A solid figure which can be packed without gaps or overlaps using n unit cubes is said to have a volume of n cubic units.	100, 101

Grade 5 Common Core State Standards for Mathematical Content

5.MD   Measurement and Data, continued

St. #	Standard	Pages in This Book
4	Measure volumes by counting unit cubes, using cubic cm, cubic in, cubic ft, and improvised units.	100, 101
5	Relate volume to the operations of multiplication and addition and solve real world and mathematical problems involving volume.	
5a	Find the volume of a right rectangular prism with whole-number side lengths by packing it with unit cubes, and show that the volume is the same as would be found by multiplying the edge lengths, equivalently by multiplying the height by the area of the base. Represent threefold whole-number products as volumes, e.g., to represent the associative property of multiplication.	106
5b	Apply the formulas $V = l \times w \times h$ and $V = b \times h$ for rectangular prisms to find volumes of right rectangular prisms with whole-number edge lengths in the context of solving real world and mathematical problems.	102, 103, 104, 105
5c	Recognize volume as additive. Find volumes of solid figures composed of two non-overlapping right rectangular prisms by adding the volumes of the non-overlapping parts, applying this technique to solve real world problems.	101, 102

Grade 5 Common Core State Standards for Mathematical Content

5.G   Geometry

St. #	Standard	Pages in This Book
	Graph points on the coordinate plane to solve real-world and mathematical problems.	
1	Use a pair of perpendicular number lines, called axes, to define a coordinate system, with the intersection of the lines (the origin) arranged to coincide with the 0 on each line and a given point in the plane located by using an ordered pair of numbers, called its coordinates. Understand that the first number indicates how far to travel from the origin in the direction of one axis, and the second number indicates how far to travel in the direction of the second axis, with the convention that the names of the two axes and the coordinates correspond (e.g., x-axis and x-coordinate, y-axis and y-coordinate).	108, 109, 110, 111, 112, 113, 114, 115, 116, 117, 118, 119, 120
2	Represent real world and mathematical problems by graphing points in the first quadrant of the coordinate plane, and interpreting coordinate values of points in the context of the situation.	108, 109, 110, 111, 112, 113, 114, 115, 116, 117, 118, 119, 120
	Classify two-dimensional figures into categories based on their properties.	
3	Understand that attributes belonging to a category of two-dimensional figures also belong to all subcategories of that category. For example, all rectangles have four right angles and squares are rectangles, so all squares have four right angles.	121, 122, 123, 124, 125, 126
4	Classify two-dimensional figures in a hierarchy based on properties.	124, 125, 126

OPERATIONS
AND
ALGEBRAIC
THINKING

Grade 5

STRANGE RACES

How would you like to take a bath in the world's fastest bathtub while it was racing off the coast of Canada? How would you like to take a nap in a racing bed? You can try these at the World Championship Bathtub Races or the Knaresborough England Bed Race. The fastest bathtub race (36 miles long) took 1 hour, 22 minutes, and 27 seconds. The winner was G. Mutton. The record-holding bed racers covered two miles, 56 yards in 12 minutes and 9 seconds.

The table shows some information about other bed and bathtub races. A mathematical expression shows the number of competitors in each kind of race over five years. Evaluate the expressions. Then use the information to answer the questions.

BATHTUB RACERS & BED RACERS
BOSCO COUNTY ANNUAL TUB & BED RACES

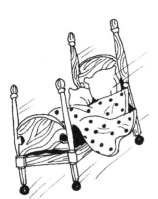

	Number of Bathtub Racers	Number of Bed Racers
Year 1	$40 \times (3 + 6)$	$16 + [5 \times (8 - 3)]$
Year 2	$6 \times [2 + (10 - 5)]$	$(3 + 17) \times (20 - 1)$
Year 3	$30 \times (9 - 4)$	$(5 \times 80) \div 2$
Year 4	$(6 + 2)^2 - 7$	$(2 + 4)^2 + 150$
Year 5	$5 \times [2 \times (6 + 9)]$	$10 \times [(8 \times 5) + 4)]$

1. How many people raced bathtubs in Year 1? _____

2. How many raced beds in Year 2? _____

3. How many raced bathtubs in Year 3? _____

4. How many raced beds in Year 4? _____

5. How many raced bathtubs in Year 5? _____

6. Which years had the same number of tub racers? _____

7. Did Year 4 have over 300 competitors total? _____

8. Which year had the greatest number of bed racers? _____

9. Which year had fewer than 50 bed racers? _____

10. How many more people raced beds in Year 3 than in Year 1? _____

Name

EXTREME LIFTING

Some of the most impressive records show great feats of strength. Imagine lifting an elephant! Oghaby of Iran holds the record for this feat. He lifted an elephant that weighed about 4,400 pounds. (By the way, he did not do this with his bare hands. He had the help of a platform and harness, but it was his strength that did the work.)

The table shows some information about six other elephant-lifters. Match numbers from the table to the expressions. Evaluate each expression. Then write the name of the elephant lifter and the Day (Day 1 or Day 2).

1. $[2 \times (1{,}000 + 300)]$ _____ _____
   name   *day*

2. $\dfrac{(10{,}000 - 1{,}800)}{2}$ _____ _____
   name   *day*

3. $3{,}000 - (600 + 200)$ _____ _____
   name   *day*

4. $10 \times [(3 \times 100) + 75]$ _____ _____
   name   *day*

5. $10 \times (100 + 30)$ _____ _____
   name   *day*

6. $(400 + 200) - 10$ _____ _____
   name   *day*

7. $(5{,}000 - 1{,}000) + 30$ _____ _____
   name   *day*

8. $(10 \times 7) \times (7 \times 10)$ _____ _____
   name   *day*

PRACTICE LIFTS

Elephant-Lifter	Day 1 Heaviest Elephant Lifted (in pounds)	Day 2 Heaviest Elephant Lifted (in pounds)
Mighty Marcos	1300	1100
Mancho Muscles	2600	4100
Stronger Samson	4030	4600
Tough Tessa	2200	3600
Bruno Bruiser	590	2600
Super Samantha	4900	3750

Name _____

LOTS OF LOOPS

In 1990, Eddy McDonald set a world record for performing the most loop-the-loop yo-yo tricks in one hour. He must have had a tired arm! His record is found in the *Guinness Book of Records.*

Read about the trick success of some other yo-yo performers. The statements tell how many loop-the-loops they did in one hour. For each performer, find the mathematical expression that matches the statement. In the expressions, "n" represents the unknown number. Write the matching expression on the line.

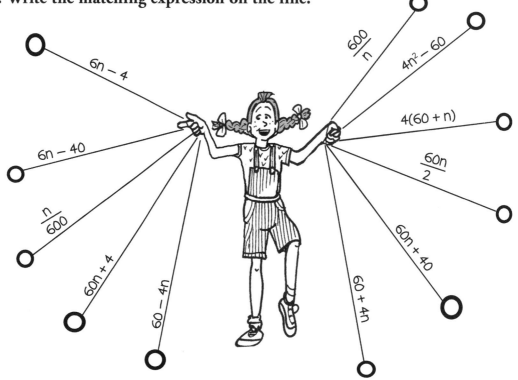

1. Yacko: sixty times a number plus forty _____

2. Yanni: six times a number of loops less forty_____

3. Yang-lei: six hundred divided by a number _____

4. Yolanda: the difference between sixty and four times a number _____

5. Yazzi: four times the sum of sixty and a number_____

6. Yuri: half of sixty times a number_____

7. Yvette: four less than six times a number _____

8. Yetty: sixty less than four times the square of a number _____

9. Yosey: four more than sixty times a number _____

10. If n = 10, which expressions show the same number of loops?_____

Name

DON'T SNEEZE!

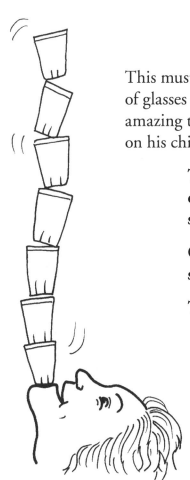

This must take years of practice. People actually balance stacks of glasses on their chins! Ashrita Furman holds the record for this amazing trick. He set the record by balancing a stack of 62 glasses on his chin for ten seconds. DON'T try this at home with real glasses!

This glass-balancer keeps practicing. The mathematical expressions described on the table below represent her successes over one week.

Complete the table. Write the expression in letters and symbols. Use *n* to represent the unknown number.

Then, evaluate each expression, using *n = 5*.

Day	Expression	Expression in Numbers and Symbols	Expression Evaluated n = 5
Sunday	nine times a number		
Monday	two less than a number		
Tuesday	six more than the square of a number		
Wednesday	half the sum of a number and 25		
Thursday	one hundred divided by a number squared		
Friday	twice the difference between 25 and a number		
Saturday	Multiply the sum of four and a number by three. Subtract ten from that.		

Name

PLAYING WITH FIRE

In 1989, Anthony Gatto of the United States set the record for flaming torch juggling. He did this by keeping seven flaming torches moving in the air at once. This is a record you should not try to match in your home or back yard!

The expressions on the torches show the number of hours Jasmine practiced torch throwing over ten months. Match each torch to one of the written statements. Write the letter of the right torch on the line.

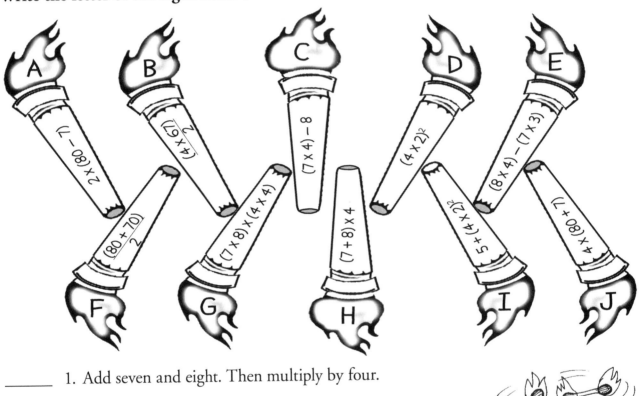

Torch A: $2 \times (80 - 7)$
Torch B: $2 \times (4 \times 9)$
Torch C: $(7 \times 4) - 8$
Torch D: $(4 \times 2)^2$
Torch E: $(8 \times 4) - (7 \times 3)$
Torch F: $\dfrac{(80 + 70)}{2}$
Torch G: $(7 \times 8) \times (4 \times 4)$
Torch H: $(7 + 8) \times 4$
Torch I: $5 + (4 \times 2)^2$
Torch J: $4 \times (80 + 7)$

_____ 1. Add seven and eight. Then multiply by four.

_____ 2. Multiply seven times four. Then subtract eight.

_____ 3. Multiply eight and four. Multiply seven and three. Find the difference between the two products.

_____ 4. Add eighty and seven. Multiply the total by four.

_____ 5. Subtract seven from eighty. Multiply the difference by two.

_____ 6. Add eighty and seventy. Divide this by two.

_____ 7. Multiply four and sixty-seven. Divide this by two.

_____ 8. Multiply four by two. Square the product.

9. Describe the expression on Torch G in words: _____

10. Describe the expression on Torch I in words: _____

Name _____

SPECTACULAR SITTING

How long could you stay in a tree or sit on a wall? Some people have done these things for a very long time. In 1997, 1998, and 1999, Julia Hill spent 728 days sitting in a tree.

Read and write these expressions that describe numbers of hours some others have taken to sit on walls or trees.

Write an expression to match the words:

1. three times the sum of twelve and fourteen _____

2. half the sum of eight, five, and nine _____

3. Add six to four. Then multiply this by six. _____

4. Divide five hundred by fifty. Then add forty-five. _____

5. Subtract the product of eight and ten from the sum of thirty and ninety. _____

Use words to match the expressions:

6. $(50 + 30) - 15$ _____

7. $16 - (10 + 20)$ _____

8. $5 \times (13 + 12)$ _____

9. $\dfrac{(55 + 21)}{2}$ _____

10. $(20 - 18) + 40$ _____

Name

Common Core Reinforcement Activities — 5th Grade Math

UNBELIEVABLE BALANCING

Arulanantham Joachim, from Sri Lanka, holds the world record for balancing on one foot. He did this for 76 hours and 40 minutes in 1997. He did not rest on his raised foot. He did not use anything to support himself.

Here are some other attempts at balancing on one foot. Choose the expression that matches the words. Circle the letter.

1. Ari

twice the sum of nineteen and thirty

  a. $2 \times (19 + 30)$ c. $(19 + 30) + 2$

  b. $(2 \times 19) + 30$ d. $2 + (19 \times 30)$

2. Mara

Multiply six and eight. Multiply seven and five. Find the difference between the products.

  a. $[(6 \times (8 \times 7 \times 5)]$ c. $(7 \times 5) \times (6 \times 8)$

  b. $(6 \times 8) + (7 \times 5)$ d. $(6 \times 8) - (7 \times 5)$

3. Ryan

half as much as twelve times nine

  a. $12 \times 9 \times 2$ c. $2 \times (12 \times 9)$

  b. $(\frac{2}{12}) \times 9$ d. $\frac{(12 \times 9)}{2}$

4. Santo

the sum of fourteen squared and six squared

  a. $(14 + 6)^2$ c. $14^2 + 6^2$

  b. $6^2 + 14$ d. $14^2 + 6$

5. Lara

Subtract fifteen from thirty-five. Add eight. Multiply the result by four.

  a. $35 - (15 + 8) \times 4$ c. $4 \times 35 - 15 + 8$

  b. $4 \times [(35 - 15) + 8)]$ d. $(35 - 15) \times (4 + 8)$

YOU write the expression for this one!

6. Rhea

Multiply ten by four. Multiply twenty by two. Find the difference between the products and multiply that by three.

Name _____

RECORD-BREAKING SNAKE SITTING

A Texas man named Jackie Bibby holds the record for sitting in a bathtub with the greatest number of poisonous snakes. There were 35 rattlesnakes. Can you imagine sitting in the tub with even one snake? Can you imagine the possibility of snakebites?

The tables show some patterns of numbers of snakes and snakebites. For each column on the table, figure out the pattern and finish filling in the table. Then answer the questions beside that table.

A

Number of Snakes	Number of Bites
0	0
3	1
6	2
9	3
12	4

1. Describe the pattern for number of snakes.
   _____

2. Describe the pattern for number of bites.
   _____

3. Describe the relationship between the patterns.
   _____

4. How many bites would you expect with 30 snakes? _____

B

Number of Snakes	Number of Bites
100	100
101	95
102	90
103	85
104	80
105	75

5. Describe the pattern for number of snakes.
   _____

6. Describe the pattern for number of bites.
   _____

7. Describe the relationship between the patterns.
   _____

8. How many bites would you expect with 50 snakes? _____

Name _____

SPECTACULAR BUBBLES

The largest bubble-gum bubble on record was 23 inches in diameter. That's almost two feet! Susan Montgomery Williams of Fresno, California blew this bubble in 1994. Measure the next bubble you blow to see how it compares!

Sasha, a middle school student, has a unique approach to bubble blowing. She finds that the size of her bubble is affected by the number of times she chews her piece of gum before blowing the bubble. The table shows the sizes of bubbles that Sasha blew in one tournament, along with the number of chews before each trial.

Look at the data for Sasha. Decide what the pattern is for each column. Then follow the patterns to finish the table.

Follow the directions on the next page to graph the patterns.

Sasha's Bubbles, June Competition

Number of Chews Before Blowing	Bubble Diameter in Inches
0	0
3	2
6	4
	6
12	
15	10

1. Describe the pattern for the number of Sasha's chews before blowing a bubble.

_____

_____

_____

Ordered Pairs
(0, 0)
(3, 2)

2. Describe the pattern for the size of Sasha's bubbles.

_____

_____

_____

3. When you have finished the table above, write an ordered number pair with terms from the same line on the table.

Use with page 27.

Name _____

Graph the information from page 26 about Sasha's bubble-blowing. Work with the ordered pairs on the small table near the bottom of the page. Your line will show how the size of her bubbles changes as the number of chews changes. After you graph the line, answer the question.

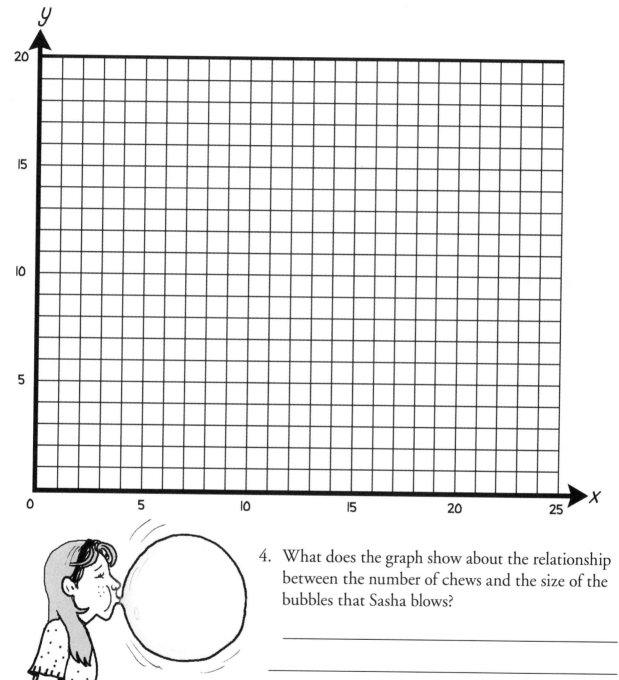

4. What does the graph show about the relationship between the number of chews and the size of the bubbles that Sasha blows?

_____

_____

_____

_____

Use with page 26.

Name _____

GIGANTIC GULPS

The largest milkshake ever made was a 4,333-gallon delight mixed up in England in 1996. Can you guess the flavor? It was strawberry. The record book does not tell who drank the shake!

The data on the Gigantic Gulps table shows the number of sips taken by milkshake drinkers in different age groups. Figure out the pattern for each column in the table. Finish the table by continuing the pattern. Then answer the questions.

Age Group of Milkshake Drinkers	Number of Sips Per Drinker
50	50
	46
44	38
42	
	30
32	

1. Describe the pattern of the milkshake drinkers' age groups.

   _____

   _____

2. Describe the pattern of the number of sips per drinker.

   _____

   _____

3. Describe the relationship between the two patterns.

   _____

   _____

4. Following this pattern, how old is a milkshake drinker who takes 6 sips?

   _____

   _____

Name

NUMBER
AND
OPERATIONS
IN
BASE TEN

Grade 5

PREPOSTEROUS CONCOCTIONS

Many people try to set records by creating or building something bigger than has ever been done before. Some of these concoctions can be eaten. Others are just wonderful to view!

The table shows some of the fascinating and surprising record-setting concoctions. Use the table and your knowledge of place value in numerals to answer the questions.

Sizes of Record-Setting Concoctions

Concoction & Record	Record Size	Concoction & Record	Record Size
biggest quiche	16 ft *diameter*	biggest pie	40 ft *diameter*
biggest hamburger	21 ft *diameter*	biggest bubblegum bubble	23 in *diameter*
biggest pizza	122 ft, 8 in *diameter*	biggest yo-yo	10 ft, 4 in *diameter*
longest sausage	2889 ft, 3 in *long*	longest salami	68 ft, 9 in *long*
tallest scarecrow	103 ft, 7 in *tall*	biggest stuffed toy	506 yd *long*
tallest sand castle	21 ft, 6 in *tall*	biggest paella	65 ft, 7 in *diameter*

WORLD'S LONGEST SAUSAGE LINK
(ENDS IN THE NEXT COUNTY)

1. Which measurement contains a number with 50 tens? _____

2. Which measurement contains a number with 21 ones? _____

3. Which measurements fall between 60 and 70 ones ? _____

4. Which measurement contains a number with 10 tens? _____

5. Which measurement contains a number with 28 hundreds? _____

6. Which measurement contains a number with 40 ones? _____

7. Which measurement contains a number with 12 tens? _____

8. Which measurement contains a number with 10 ones? _____

9. Which measurements contain numbers with 7 ones? _____

10. In the sausage measurement, how many tens are represented by the first 8 from the left? _____

Use with page 31.

Name

**Here are more questions about large creations.
Write or circle an answer for each question.**

11. The gigantic hamburger was shared by 1,698 eaters.

    How many hundreds
    are represented by the 1? _____

12. The huge scarecrow has
    frightened away 42,966 birds.

    How many hundreds are
    in this number? (Circle one.)

    42   429   96   29

13. The salami was sliced into 6,080 slices.

    How many tens are
    represented by the 6? _____

14. It took 135,216 buckets of sand
    to build the sand castle.

    How many thousands
    are represented by the 3? _____

15. The biggest paella contained 9,315 shellfish.

    How many hundreds are in this number? (Circle one.)

    31   315   931   93

16. It took 1,079 eggs to make the quiche.

    How many ones are represented by the 7?_____

17. 1,836 people shared the pizza.

    How many tens are represented by the 8? _____

18. The biggest yo-yo needed 286 feet of string.

    How many ones are represented by the 2?_____

Use with page 30.

Name _____

©Incentive Publications, Inc., Nashville, TN

Common Core Reinforcement Activities — 5th Grade Math

LOADS OF LITTER

One day a huge number of collectors gathered to pick up litter in one place. There were 50,405 people who worked to pick up litter on the California coast. This set a record for the most litter collectors.

Each bag contains a load of litter. Answer each question about the numbers of litter items in the bags. Write the letter of the bag and the number.

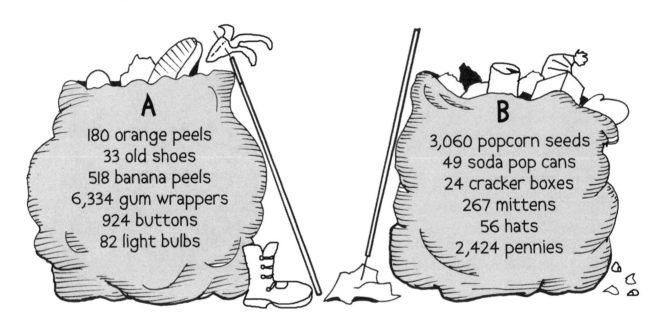

A
180 orange peels
33 old shoes
518 banana peels
6,334 gum wrappers
924 buttons
82 light bulbs

B
3,060 popcorn seeds
49 soda pop cans
24 cracker boxes
267 mittens
56 hats
2,424 pennies

	bag	the number

The number has

1. 26 tens   _____ _____

2. 24 hundreds   _____ _____

3. 33 tens   _____ _____

4. 18 ones   _____ _____

5. 18 tens   _____ _____

6. 4 tens   _____ _____

7. 56 ones   _____ _____

	bag	the number

The number has

8. 90 tens   _____ _____

9. 30 hundreds   _____ _____

10. 180 ones   _____ _____

11. 33 ones   _____ _____

12. 80 ones   _____ _____

13. 633 tens   _____ _____

14. 242 tens   _____ _____

Name _____

LIGHT? OR NO LIGHT?

Six hundred thousand light bulbs would give off a lot of light! This is the number of bulbs in Hugh Hicks' collection. He's been gathering light bulbs since childhood, and now has the world's largest collection. Is it possible they all still work?

The number 600,000 has five zeros.
It is a product of 60 times ten five times (60 x 10 x 10 x 10 x 10 x 10).
This can be stated as 60 times 10 to the fifth power or 60×10^5.

Follow the directions to multiply by powers of ten.

1. Assume that four of every six light bulbs
   in Hicks' collection are burned out. This would be
   four hundred thousand or 4×10^4. Write this number: _____

2. In City A, 3×10^7 lights are turned on
   in homes and on streets. Write this number: _____

3. In City B, 90,000 lights were turned on at dark.
   Write this number as a power of ten. _____

4. City C has 10,000 times as many lights burning as
   City D. City D has 6,431 lights burning. How many
   zeros will be in the number of lights burning in City D? _____

5. In City X, 540,000,000 lights are burning.
   Which number is this? (Circle one.)

   54×10^9 54×10^8 54×10^7 540×10^5 54×10^6

Circle one answer.

6. Which is the product of 116 and 10^5?

   a. 11,600   b. 116,000   c. 11,600,000

7. Which is the product of 10^4 and 15?

   a. 15,000   b. 150,000   c. 1,500,000

8. Which is the product of 50, 2, and 10^3?

   a. 1,000   b. 10,000   c. 100,000

Name _____

THE BIGGEST DROP

Frenchman Michel Menin walked high above the countryside in France to set the record for highest tightrope walk. The drop stretched above a 10,335-foot drop. Fortunately, Michel did not drop off the rope.

The table below contains numbers that will help you find the heights of the ropes across which some tightrope walkers practiced. Use the table and follow instructions on page 35 to find these drops.

Tightrope-Walking Trials
Tightrope Heights in Feet

Competitor	Trial 1	Trial 2	Trial 3
Martina	2.7361	122.41	19.54
Mario	410.01	66.5	808.088
Misha	28.67	699.9	0.0115
Michelle	532.1	0.861	10.01
Martin	4.6	7770.7	7.77
Manuel	3.966	5473	0.0009
Maddy	1,931.05	0.013	168.853

Use with page 35.

Name

Use the information from the table on page 34 to solve the problems.

1. Multiply Martina's first trial by 10^3 (2.7361×10^3).

    What happens to the decimal point? _____

    What is the answer? Height of the rope is _____ ft.

2. Divide Mario's first trial by 10^2 ($410.01 \div 10^2$).

    What happens to the decimal point? _____

    What is the answer? Height of the rope is _____ ft.

The longest tightrope walk lasted 205 days. An amazing performer, Jorge Ojeda-Guzman, spent all this time dancing and walking and balancing a chair on the tightrope that was 35 feet above the ground. You can imagine how much fun this was for the spectators!

It's been a long day.

Write the new distance in feet.

3. Martina, Trial 2 x 10 = _____

4. Martina, Trial 3 ÷ 10 = _____

5. Mario, Trial 2 x 10^2 = _____

6. Mario, Trial 3 ÷ 10^3 = _____

7. Misha, Trial 1 ÷ 10^3 = _____

8. Misha, Trial 2 x 10^2 = _____

9. Misha, Trial 3 x 10^5 = _____

10. Michelle, Trial 1 ÷ 10^2 = _____

11. Michelle, Trial 2 x 10^4 = _____

12. Michelle, Trial 3 x 10^2 = _____

13. Martin, Trial 1 x 10^3 = _____

14. Martin, Trial 2 ÷ 10^4 = _____

15. Martin, Trial 3 x 10^3 = _____

16. Manuel, Trial 1 x 10^2 = _____

17. Manuel, Trial 2 x 10^3 = _____

18. Manuel, Trial 3 x 10^7 = _____

19. Maddy, Trial 1 ÷ 10^5 = _____

20. Maddy, Trial 2 x 10^5 = _____

Use with page 34.

Name

INCREDIBLE CREATIONS

A team in British Columbia built the tallest sand castle. Team members used only their hands, shovels, and pails to build the 21-foot, 6-inch high castle.

The teams shown below spent a week building castles. Solve problems about their work.

1. The *Sand Wizards* worked 1000 times .0706 hours = _____.

2. The *Sculptors* traveled this far to the competition: 8,700 miles ÷ 10 = _____.

3. The *Builders Four* used this many shovels and other tools: $53,000 ÷ 10^3$ = _____.

4. The *Castle Quartet* worked 3,600,000 hours ÷ 10^5 = _____.

5. The *Sand Crabs* drank this much water during the time they worked:

   0.0114 liters x 10^5 = _____.

6. This many birds flew over the sand castle builders during the week-long competition:

   0.001746 x 10^6 = _____.

7. This many spectators came
   to see the sand creations:

   402,600,000 ÷ 10^5 = _____.

8. The total number of hours worked
   by the builders was:

   66,200,000,000 ÷ 10^8 hours = _____.

Sand Castle Contest
Number of Buckets of Sand Used for Creations

The table gives a mathematical multiplication or division problem that will show the number of buckets of sand used for each castle. Solve the problems.

Team	Perform the Operation	Answer
The Sand Wizards	0.0247 x 10^5	
The Sand Crabs	37,000,000 ÷ 10^4	
The Builders Four	0.0046 x 10^6	
The Sculptors	93,266,000 ÷ 10^5	
The Castle Quartet	0.0024566 x 10^6	

Name _____

WHAT A RIDE!

The speediest wheelbarrow racing record was set in South Africa in 1987. Someone pushed a wheelbarrow holding a rider one mile in 4 minutes and 48.51 seconds.

This time in seconds is 288.51 seconds.

This number can be shown as
$(2 \times 100) + (8 \times 10) + (8 \times 1) + (5 \times \frac{1}{10}) + \frac{1}{100}$.

Write these times as expanded numerals.

1. One-mile race—time: 125.68 sec.

   _____

2. Five-mile race—time: 1,300.85 sec.

   _____

3. Ten-mile race—time: 2,200.24 sec.

   _____

4. Tenth-mile—time: 16.051 sec.

   _____

5. Ten-kilometer race—time: 1,008.005 sec.

   _____

6. 100-meter: 55.079 sec.

   _____

Write these times as decimal numerals.

7. $(3 \times 1000) + (3 \times 100) + 8 + \frac{3}{100}$ _____

8. $(6 \times 1000) + (2 \times 10) + (5 \times \frac{1}{100}) + (2 \times \frac{1}{1000})$ _____

9. $(4 \times 10,000) + (5 \times 100) + (9 \times \frac{1}{10}) + (8 \times \frac{1}{1000})$ _____

Name _____

A WHOLE LOT OF PIGS

It has taken Ove Nordstrom forty years to build his record-setting collection of piggy banks. He now has 3,575 pig-shaped containers that hold money!

Maybe Ove's banks were full of coins! These problems use words to describe weights of different full banks. For each one, circle the decimal number that matches the written weight.

1 two hundred five and
one hundred six thousandths

    a. 25.016

    b. 205.106

    c. 205.16

    d. 200.516

2 three thousand seventeen
ten thousandths

    a. 0.3017

    b. 3.017

    c. 0.317

    d. 0.30017

3 sixty and six thousandths

    a. 60.6006

    b. 60.66

    c. 66.06

    d. 60.006

4 one thousand and
one hundred and one thousandths

    a. 1000.011

    b. 0.1101

    c. 0.0111

    d. 1000.101

5 three and three thousand
three ten thousandths

    a. 3.303

    b. 3.3003

    c. 3.33

    d. 3.3033

Use with page 39.

Name

These problems use words to describe weights of different full banks.
For each one, circle the decimal number that matches the written weight.

6

sixteen and
ninety-four
thousandths

a. 16.094
b. 1.6094
c. 16.904
d. 0.16094

9

twenty-two and
twenty-two
thousandths

a. 0.2222
b. 22.022
c. 22.202
d. 22.220

7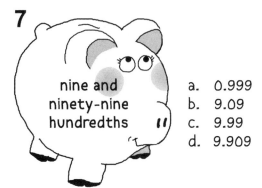

nine and
ninety-nine
hundredths

a. 0.999
b. 9.09
c. 9.99
d. 9.909

10

four hundred four
ten
thousandths

a. 4.04
b. 0.0404
c. 0.404
d. 400.0001

8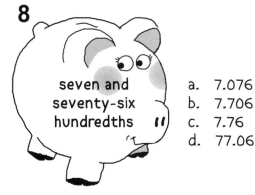

seven and
seventy-six
hundredths

a. 7.076
b. 7.706
c. 7.76
d. 77.06

11

twelve and
seven
thousandths

a. 0.1207
b. 12.0007
c. 12.7000
d. 12.007

Use with page 38.

Name

WALKING TALL

The longest walk on stilts covered 3,008 miles. In 1980, Joe Bowen walked from California to Kentucky. The tallest stilts ever used for a walk measured over 40 feet tall. In 1988, Travix Wolf walked 26 steps on these.

A group of kids decided to walk on stilts to raise money for their community food bank. The problems show some of the distances they walked (in meters).

Write each number in words.

1. 3.72 _____

_____

2. 2.604 _____

_____

3. 0.59 _____

4. 9.98 _____

5. 7.002 _____

6. 9.09 _____

7. 10.015 _____

8. 1.5 _____

9. 8.35 _____

Use numerals to write each number.

10. twelve and forty-four hundredths _____

11. seven hundred eight thousandths _____

12. forty-four and twenty-two hundredths _____

Name _____

AN "EGG"-CELLENT RECORD

It is quite a trick to balance one egg on a ledge or on the edge of a table. Imagine how difficult it must be to balance 210 eggs at the same time! This is the record for egg balancing by one person. Kenneth Epperson of Georgia set this record in 1990.

Check out the "balance" between the two eggs in each row. How do the numbers compare? Write <, >, or = in each square to complete a true statement about the two decimal numbers.

1 15.15 ☐ 15.51

2 0.22 ☐ 0.92

3 1.33 ☐ 1.330

4 5.084 ☐ 5.101

5 10.01 ☐ 10.009

6 0.512 ☐ 0.509

7 10.05 ☐ 10.050

8 0.4106 ☐ 0.4016

Name

Common Core Reinforcement Activities — 5th Grade Math

RECORD-SETTING SWALLOWING

In an attempt to set food-eating records, some people swallow large amounts of food in extremely fast times. Pancakes, spaghetti, raw eggs, whole lemons, pickled onions, and other interesting foods are gobbled up for the sake of competition.

Read the statements about some competitive eaters. Write a competitor's name, or the word *neither*, to answer each question. (The food items in each category were all the same size.)

1. Amy ate 12.3 raw eggs. Andy ate 12.03 cooked eggs.

   Who ate the most? _____

2. Bo ate 28.065 hot dogs. Moe ate 28.506 hot dogs.

   Who ate the most? _____

3. J.R. ate 6.002 pounds of sausage. T.J. ate 6.020 pounds.

   Who ate the most? _____

4. Tisha ate 14.099 bananas. Thomas ate 14.1 bananas.

   Who ate the most? _____

5. Lars ate 3.05 lemons. Lara ate 3.055 lemons.

   Who ate the most? _____

6. Kimo ate 22.08 kippers. Kanya ate 22.0078 kippers.

   Who ate the most? _____

7. Max ate 2.015 meters of spaghetti. Tex ate 2.018 meters.

   Who ate the most? _____

8. Don ate 20.303 hamburgers. Danya ate 20.333 hamburgers.

   Who ate the most? _____

9. Lou ate 7.08 pizzas. Sue ate 7.0080 pizzas.

   Who ate the most? _____

10. Ari ate 5.09 pickled onions. Mari ate 5.090 pickled onions.

    Who ate the most? _____

Use with page 43.

Name

Compare Decimals

Read the statements about some competitive eaters. Write a competitor's name, or the word *neither*, to answer each question. (The food items in each category were all the same size.)

11. Axel ate 17.5 avocados. Roxy ate 17.52. Who ate the most? _____	12. Al ate 13.7 tacos. Sal ate 13.07. Who ate the least? _____	13. Ed ate 1.4 raw onions. Fred ate 1.44. Who ate the most? _____
14. George ate 9.106 pounds of baked beans. Georgia ate 9.660 pounds. Who ate the most? _____	15. DeShaun ate 27.050 pickles. DeAnne ate 27.05. Who ate the least? _____	16. Lucy ate 4.35 bagels. Lexi ate 4.53. Who ate the most? _____
17. Will ate a pizza in 87.087 seconds. Bill ate a pizza in 87.0870 seconds. Who ate the fastest? _____	18. Chen drank a milkshake in 27.001 seconds. Lin drank a milkshake in 26.999 seconds. Who drank fastest? _____	19. Charlie ate 4.444 jalapenos in one minute. Charlene ate 4.49 jalapenos in one minute. Who ate the least? _____

Use with page 42.

Name

43

TATTOOS, KISSES, AND SUCH

Which record do you wish you had set—the highest hot air balloon flight, the most ice cream eaten, the fastest bathtub race, the deepest ocean dive, the longest distance for spitting a cricket, the longest kiss, the longest time spent living with scorpions—or something else?

Hundreds of kids were asked this question. See this page and the next page for their top 20 answers. Then follow the directions to round the decimal numerals about some distances, times, and amounts.

We tried to set the record for the highest hot air balloon flight . . .

. . . but we broke the record for ice-cream eating!

Yum!

Records I Wish I Had Set
Top Ten Favorite Records

Highest Hot Air Balloon Ride
Fastest Talker
Longest Dance
Most Time Living in a Tree
Longest Fingernails
Longest Lawnmower Ride
Longest High-Wire Walk
Shortest Time to Eat a Raw Onion
Longest Kiss
Fastest Run Wearing
    a Darth Vader Costume

1. Danielle and Dionne rode the rollercoaster for 5.42 hours.

   Round this to the nearest tenth of an hour. _____

2. Adriana and Louis danced for 12.408 hours.

   Round this to the nearest hundredth of an hour. _____

3. Daria talked nonstop for 10.353 hours.

   Round this to the nearest tenth of an hour. _____

4. Kohann lived in a tree for 3.75 years.

   Round this to the nearest tenth of a year. _____

5. Pierre rode a lawnmower 258.608 miles.

   Round this to the nearest hour. _____

6. Savannah grew fingernails 0.3375 meters long.

   Round this to the nearest thousandth of a meter. _____

7. Adriana and Louis danced for 12.408 hours.

   Round this to the nearest hundredth of an hour. _____

8. Carlos and Gianna did a 1,500.69-meter tandem tightrope walk.

   Round this to the nearest meter. _____

Use with page 45.

Name

Hundreds of kids were asked this question: *What world record do you wish you had set?*
Here are the rest of their answers.
Finish page 44. Then follow the directions to round the decimal numerals about some distances, times, and amounts.

Records I Wish I Had Set
Next Ten Favorite Records

Most Pancakes Eaten in an Hour
Greatest Number of Tattoos
Largest Pizza Tossed
Longest Walk on Hands
Tallest Birthday Cake
Longest Bumper Car Marathon
Longest Barefoot Water-ski
Most Pickled Eggs Eaten
Largest Snowman Built
Longest Motorcycle Jump

9. Layla ate 39.2062 pancakes in one hour.

   Round this to the nearest hundredth of an hour. _____

10. Josiah has tattoos on 0.605 of his body surface.

    Round this to the nearest tenth. _____

11. MacKenzie built a snowman 3.007 meters tall.

    Round this to the nearest tenth of a meter. _____

12. Anthony walked on his hands for 2.685 kilometers.

    Round this to the nearest hundredth of a kilometer. _____

13. Destiny ate 30.06 pickled eggs in an hour.

    Round this to the nearest tenth of an egg. _____

14. Morgan ran 2,500.075 meters wearing a Darth Vadar costume.

    Round this to the nearest tenth of a meter. _____

15. Juan and Jayden rode a bumper car for 78.05 hours.

    Round this to the nearest hour. _____

16. Carson tossed a 75.0788-centimeter diameter pizza.

    Round this to the nearest thousandth of a centimeter. _____

Use with page 44.

Name

RECORD-SETTING DREAMS

What does it take to set a record? It takes imagination, time, patience, and a lot of work. Some of the records take plenty of skill or money, too! In addition, you might need to do some research if you want to try for a record.

Here is the library of Dominic, a future record-setter. He is busily reading all these books because he dreams of setting some new records. In each statement, find a number of pages Dominic has finished. Round the number to the bold place. Circle the correctly-rounded number.

1. Dominic read **55.7**5 pages in *Pancake Tossing*.

    55.7   55.8   56   55

2. Dominic is fascinated with the idea of eating a car. He read 130.**2**85 pages of *Car Eating*.

    130.3   130.29   130.28   130.2

3. After winning a forward race. Dominic scanned 62.**9**9 pages of *Backward Racing*.

    62.9   62.09   62   63

4. Dominic read **12**.76 pages of *Collecting Parking Meters* to compare his collection to others' collections.

    12.01   12.1   12   13

5. Before breakfast, Dominic read 9.**9**52 pages in *Egg Balancing*.

    10   9.9   9.95   9.0

6. Dominic and his pet frog looked through 30.**8**66 pages in *Leapfrogging*.

    31   30.8   30.9   30.87

7. Dominic read **105**.095 pages in *Unicycle Racing* before buying a unicycle.

    105.9   105   105.1   106

8. After reading **1**49.94 pages in *Fast Shaving*, Dominic decided not to try this sport.

    149.9   150   140   200   100

I ATE THAT BOOK IN RECORD TIME!

Name

ENORMOUS EDIBLES

ENORMOUS CAKES

Cake Baker	Number of Layers
Pierre Pastry	63
Chef B. Aker	42
Francine F. Frosting	59
Daniel D. Sert	47
ChiChi Choco Late	66
Yolanda Yum	29
Iris I. Sing	42
Gustavus Goodie	38
Valerie Vanilla	52
Cassandra Calorie	42
Tyra Misu	27

It took 20 chefs in China over 24 hours to make the world's tallest cake. Standing at eight meters tall, it had eight layers and weighed about 2,000 kilograms. Imagine how much fun it would be to help eat that cake!

Look at the data about the cakes in another contest. Use those numbers to solve the multiplication problems.

1. Which baker created a cake with about twice the layers of Yolanda Yum's cake?

   Answer: _____

2. It took Gustavus Goodie 12 minutes to place and ice each layer. How long did it take him to put the cake together?

   Answer: _____

3. What is the product of the number of layers for the cakes of Iris I. Sing and Daniel D. Sert?

   Answer: _____

4. Chef B. Aker used 3 eggs per layer of his cake. How many eggs did he use?

   Answer: _____

5. Valerie Vanilla used 50 vanilla sprinkles on top of each layer. How many sprinkles did she use?

   Answer: _____

6. Fourteen people enjoyed eating each layer of Tyra Misu's delicious tiramisu-flavored cake. How many people joined in eating the whole cake?

   Answer: _____

7. Cassandra Calorie figured out that each layer of her cake contained 276 calories. How many calories were contained in the entire cake?

   Answer: _____

8. Chef ChiChi Choco Late baked 87 chocolate chips into each layer of her cake. How many chocolate chips would be found in the whole cake?

   Answer: _____

9. In chef school, Pierre Pastry learned to use plenty of butter. Each layer of his cake contained 9 ounces of butter. How much butter was in the whole cake?

   Answer: _____

Name

OUTRAGEOUS COLLECTIONS

What strange things some people collect! Many people have collections, but some take it to extremes. People who collect thousands of magnets, clovers, mousetraps, or airsickness bags may do this for the love of collecting. Or they may do it to get in the record books!

Look at the data for some outrageous collections. Use those numbers to solve the multiplication problems. Write *yes* or *no* for each question.

OUTRAGEOUS COLLECTIONS

Collection	Collector	Record Number Collected
mousetraps	Reinhard Hellwig	2,334
golf balls	Ted J. Hoz	43,824
items of underwear	Imelda Marcos	1,700
shoes	Sonja Bata	10,000
watches	Florenzo Barindelli	3,562
light bulbs	Hugh Hicks	60,000
airsickness bags	Nick Vermeulen	2,112
gnomes & pixies	Anne Atkin	2,010
bandages (unused)	Brian Viner	3,750
refrigerator magnets	Louise J. Greenfarb	21,500
clovers	George Kaminski	13,382 four-leaf 1,336 five-leaf 78 six-leaf 6 seven-leaf
bubble gum	Thomas & Volker Martins	1,712
parking meters	Lotta Sjölin	292
nutcrackers	Jürgen Löschner	2,200
ballpoint pens	Angelika Unverhau	108,500
piggy banks	Ove Nortstrom	3,575
jet fighters	Michel Pont	100
marbles	Sam McCarthy-Fox	40,000

_____ 1. Is the ballpoint pen collection about three times the size of the watch collection?

_____ 2. Hugh Hicks has broken four light bulbs for every bulb he has been able to save in the collection. Has he broken 24,000 bulbs?

_____ 3. Did Sam McCarthy-Fox collect 4,000 times as many items as Michel Pont?

_____ 4. If each of Ove Nortstrom's piggy banks contains $45 worth of coins, does he have $160,875 in his banks?

_____ 5. Reinhard Hellwig has caught 25 mice in each of his mousetraps. Does this amount to 68,500 mice?

_____ 6. Ted J. Hoz swings an average of three times each time he tries to hit a golf ball. If he hits each ball in his collection, he figures he would take about 13,000 swings. Is he correct?

_____ 7. George Kaminski hopes to triple his collection of four-leaf clovers. He thinks this will give him about 50,000 of the clovers. Is he correct?

_____ 8. A neighbor of Sonja Bata has collected 250 shoes. Sonja thinks she has 40 times as many shoes as her neighbor. Is she correct?

_____ 9. If you could collect 15 times the number of refrigerator magnets as Louise Greenfarb, would you have half a million magnets?

_____ 10. Thomas and Volker Martins think five times their collection is a number greater than four times the number of Nick Vermeullen's airsickness bags. Are they correct?

Use with page 49.

Name

OUTRAGEOUS COLLECTIONS, continued

Curious visitors come to see many of the record-setting collections listed on page 48. Here is some data about visitors to other collections that have not set any records. Use those numbers to solve the multiplication problems. Write *yes* or *no* for each question.

CURIOUS VISITORS
Numbers of Visitors May-June

Collection Visited	May	June	July	August
Elvis souvenirs	666	900	1,001	768
ski poles	89	320	465	345
shoes	1,000	1,590	1,899	1,200
marbles	707	933	955	700
safety pins	30	66	71	14
stuffed animals	4,500	4,811	5,736	4,801
spoons	691	699	741	366
gum wrappers	190	580	711	533
cash registers	1,101	2,801	4,138	3,100
lightbulbs	1,400	1,451	1,478	1,410
shoelaces	57	84	99	150

_____ 11. The visitors to the collection of Elvis souvenirs in May saw 10 times as many souvenirs as there were visitors in that month. Did they see 66,600 souvenirs?

_____ 12. The visitors to the safety pin exhibit saw a variety of 1,850 safety pins. Julie has her own collection of twice that many. Is her collection over 4,000 safety pins?

_____ 13. Twelve times as many visitors saw the gum wrapper collection in September as in August. Was this number 6,396?

_____ 14. In May through August, three times as many visitors saw the stuffed animals as visited the collection in April. Did the April group total 7,208?

_____ 15. 495 people viewed the shoelace exhibit in September. The owner of the collection thought this number of visitors was five times July's number. Was she correct?

_____ 16. Is four times the number of May cash register visitors greater than ten times the June visitors to the ski pole collection?

_____ 17. Did eight times as many people visit the shoe exhibit in August as visited the shoelace exhibit in the same month?

_____ 18. Is there a collection that had a number of visitors (in any month) equal to about 4 times the number who visited the marble display in August?

Use with page 48.

Name _____

OUTLANDISH COMPETITIONS

There are some very strange competitions out there! It is quite amazing what things people think of to eat, balance, throw, juggle, build, and race! Here are a few of the real things people do for fun to try to set new records for how many, how long, or how far they can do something.

The table shows the number of competitors for each of four years at some of these strange competitions. Use the information from the table to answer the questions.

WATERMELON SEED SPITTING ROOM 12

Wild & Wacky Competitions
Frequency of Registrations

Competition	Year 1	Year 2	Year 3	Year 4
Pizza Tossers	53	18	45	50
Watermelon Seed Spitters	4	9	26	35
Onion Eaters	14	22	46	17
Elephant Lifters	3	2	0	8
Egg Balancers	27	6	19	9
Bubble Blowers	31	17	14	13
Mosquito Killers	2	5	8	11
Wall Sitters	10	6	12	5
Lemon Eaters	5	15	20	30
Bed Makers	3	10	15	16
Shoe Shiners	26	4	19	12
Sand Castle Builders	10	20	35	46
Flaming Torch Jugglers	0	0	8	5

1. Which competition had a number of registrations greater than twice the number of watermelon seed spitters in Year 3?

   Answer: _____

2. In which year did the bubble blowers have a number half that of another number of registrations on the table?

   Answer: _____

3. After Year 4, mosquito killing jumped in popularity. Fourteen times as many people competed in Year 5 as in Year 4. How many was this?

   Answer: _____

4. In a year not shown, 729 people registered to balance eggs. This is 27 times the number in which year of egg balancing?

   Answer: _____

5. The shoe shiners registered in Year 3 each brought 18 kinds of shoe polish. How many containers of shoe polish were on hand that year?

   Answer: _____

6. In the fifth year, 414 onion eaters showed up. This is nine times the number in what other year?

   Answer: _____

Use with page 51.

Name

More and more people try to set or break world-wide or local records. Solve the problems about record-setting attempts.

7. A pair of pizza-tossers flung one pizza dough that was 88 inches in diameter. This was 4 times the size of another pizza dough in the competition. What was the size of the smaller one? Answer: _____

8. A champion elephant lifter was so proud of herself for being able to lift the big elephants. She held a 2,256-pound animal aloft for 15 seconds. This was twelve times the weight lifted by her closest competitor. How much did the other elephant weigh? Answer: _____

9. A lemon eater had practiced for weeks before the competition. During the competition, she ate 12 lemons. In practice, she consumed 48 times that many over a period of 16 weeks. How many did she eat in practice? Answer: _____

10. Michel the Magnificent juggled flaming torches. To keep his arms strong, he did a lot of pushups. Before a performance in which he juggled torches for 26 minutes, he had done 22 times that many pushups. What was the number of pushups?
    Answer: _____

11. Sam and his friend Pam were super-fast bed makers. They could put sheets, blankets, and pillowcases on in record time. They made 164 beds in 2,132 seconds. What was the average time for each bed?
    Answer: _____

12. Camille sat on a wall without any support for 184 hours. Carlos sat on the same wall without support for 16 times that long. How long did Carlos sit?
    Answer: _____

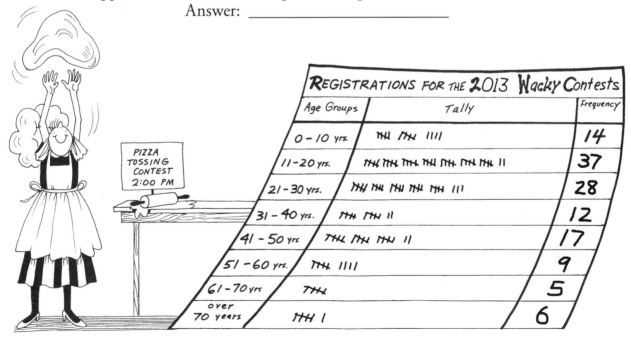

Use with page 50.

Name

DO YOU TATTOO?

BIKER BOB'S
BARBEQUE
CAFE

To break this record, you would need to get most of your body covered with tattoos. The record for the most tattoos is held by Bernie Moeller, who has 14,006 individual tattoos.

Solve the tattoo problems. Briefly describe the strategy you used to solve each problem.

1. If Bernie Moeller got 94 tattoos every month, how many months would it have taken him to get all 14,006 tattoos?

   Answer: _____ Strategy: _____

   _____

2. At Biker Bob's Cafe, 375 of today's 500 customers had tattoos. This was 25 times the number of waiters and waitresses with tattoos. How many waiters or waitresses had tattoos?

   Answer: _____ Strategy: _____

   _____

3. 60,000 ÷ 12

   Answer: _____ Strategy: _____

   _____

4. 8,830 ÷ 70

   Answer: _____ Strategy: _____

   _____

5. 5,047 ÷ 49

   Answer: _____ Strategy: _____

   _____

6. 8844 ÷ 11

   Answer: _____ Strategy: _____

   _____

7. One-eighth of twelve hundred twenty-four

   Answer: _____ Strategy: _____

   _____

8. 630,000 ÷ 90

   Answer: _____ Strategy: _____

   _____

Name _____

TO CATCH A BOOMERANG

It may sound easy to catch a boomerang after you've thrown it away. But if you've tried it, you know that it takes skill and practice! At the Indoor Boomerang Throwing Competition in 1998, an Englishman set a new record. Lawrence West threw and caught a boomerang 20 times in one minute.

Another boomerang catcher has kept a record of her highest number of catches each week over a period of ten weeks. Use the information to write and solve the problems.

Best Record
For Each Week

Week	Number Caught
1	3
2	6
3	9
4	7
5	9
6	16
7	13
8	17
9	21
10	16

Week 1: missed 47 times as many as caught—How many missed? _____

Week 2: missed 40 times as many as caught—How many missed? _____

Week 3: missed 62 times as many as caught—How many missed? _____

Week 4: missed 48 times as many as caught—How many missed? _____

Week 5: missed 35 times as many as caught—How many missed? _____

Week 6: missed 30 times as many as caught—How many missed? _____

Week 7: missed 22 times as many as caught—How many missed? _____

Week 8: missed 13 times as many as caught—How many missed? _____

Week 9: missed 11 times as many as caught—How many missed? _____

Week 10: missed 6 times as many as caught—How many missed? _____

Name

A PUZZLING RECORD

The largest jigsaw puzzle that was successfully finished contained 43,924 pieces. Imagine how long it took to put this one together!

Mariah finds several jars. Each one contains pieces for a puzzle. She grabs a handful of pieces from one jar. Amazingly, the total number of pieces in that puzzle is a multiple of the number in her hand. This happens with every jar! Even more surprising, each time she draws a handful of pieces, if she multiplies the number by 145, the product is the number of pieces in that puzzle!

For each problem, use division to find the number of pieces she grabbed from each jar.

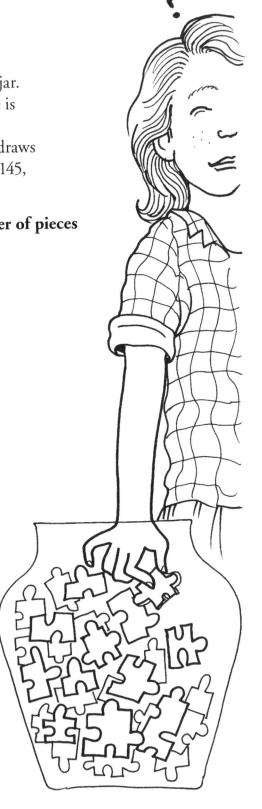

Jar # 1: _____ x 145 = 1,015

Jar # 2: _____ x 145 = 1,305

Jar # 3: _____ x 145 = 1,740

Jar # 4: _____ x 145 = 725

Jar # 5: _____ x 145 = 870

Jar # 6: _____ x 145 = 2,030

Jar # 7: _____ x 145 = 1,160

Jar # 8: _____ x 145 = 1,885

Jar # 9: _____ x 145 = 2,175

Jar # 10: _____ x 145 = 1,595

Name

SPEEDY PUZZLING

In 2012, Elaine Lewis, of the UK, finished a 250-piece puzzle in 14 minutes, 58 seconds to set a world record for the fastest puzzle completion.

In each pair of puzzle pieces here, there is a problem to solve. Perform the operation to find an answer. Think about how you solved the problem. Write a brief explanation on the blank puzzle piece.

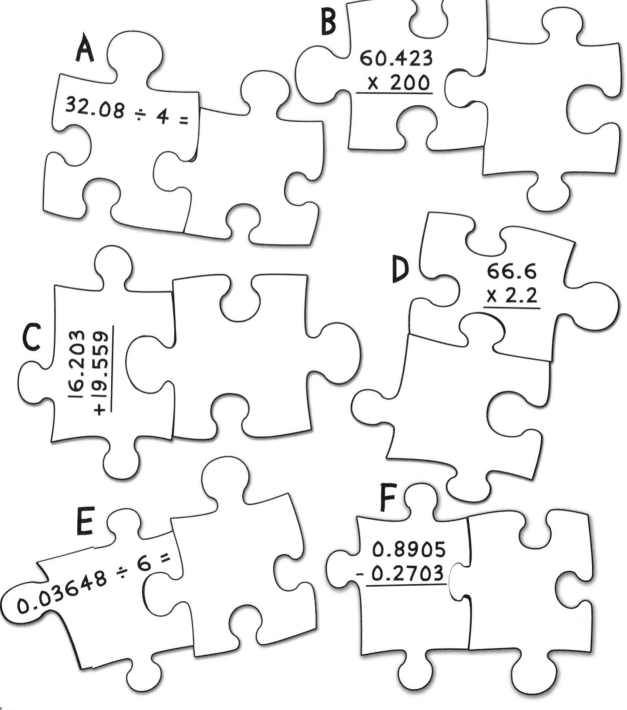

A

$32.08 \div 4 =$

B

$\begin{array}{r} 60.423 \\ \times\ 200 \\ \hline \end{array}$

C

$\begin{array}{r} 16.203 \\ +19.559 \\ \hline \end{array}$

D

$\begin{array}{r} 66.6 \\ \times\ 2.2 \\ \hline \end{array}$

E

$0.03648 \div 6 =$

F

$\begin{array}{r} 0.8905 \\ -0.2703 \\ \hline \end{array}$

Name

Common Core Reinforcement Activities — 5th Grade Math

LONG-DISTANCE CRICKET SPITTING

sploot!

Yes! People spit crickets for fun and sport! At a three-day insect celebration during the annual Bug Bowl, competitors see who can spit dead crickets the farthest. The record belongs to Danny Caps, who projected a cricket 32 feet, $\frac{1}{2}$ inch.

Here is some cricket-spitting data from a competition. Use the information for the problems below.

Cricket - Spitting Data

competitor's name	distance in feet
Lance	22.03
Fran	16.15
Sam	11.001
Van	25.4
Stan	31.05
Pam	106.10

1. What is the difference between Lance's distance and Sam's? _____

2. Stan's distance shown here is 6.11 times his first try. What was his first distance? _____

3. What is the total of all the distances shown? _____

4. On this day, Fran's distance was 6.09 feet less than her best try. What was her best try? _____

5. Alas! Pam's cricket was not dead after all! The distance shown is so great because, after Pam spit the cricket, it hopped five times farther than her spitting difference! What was her spitting distance? _____

6. How much farther did Pam's cricket travel than Van's? _____

7. The next day, Lance spit a cricket 13.904 feet more than the distance shown above. What was that new distance? _____

8. Because Pam's cricket was alive, she had to take a second try (with a different, certifiably dead cricket). This distance was 30.675 ft. What is the difference between this and the distance on the data table? _____

Use with page 57.

Name

Operations with Decimals

Follow each cricket to a problem. Solve the problem. Write a sentence or phrase telling what you did to solve it.

A

$100.001 \times 0.3 =$

B

$90.005 \div 5 =$

C

$$\begin{array}{r} 0.222 \\ \times\ \ 4.4 \\ \hline \end{array}$$

D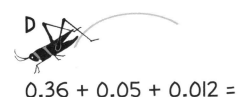

$0.36 + 0.05 + 0.012 =$

E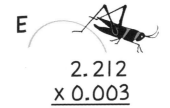

$$\begin{array}{r} 2.212 \\ \times\ 0.003 \\ \hline \end{array}$$

F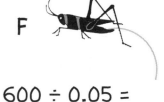

$600 \div 0.05 =$

G

twice the sum of
10.2 and 15.02

H

twelve hundredths
less than 25

I

difference between
8.036 and 9.107

Use with page 56.

Name

HOT FEET

It may sound unbelievable—walking on hot plates. You may never want to try it! (But then, maybe you will. Just don't try it at home. You would need to consult an expert.) Ron Iven of Germany set a record in 2009 for the longest distance walked on hot plates. He covered 22.9 meters.

Help this brave guy get across the hot plates quickly. Color a path with decimal problems that are correctly solved. Then go back and fix the answers to any that are not correct.

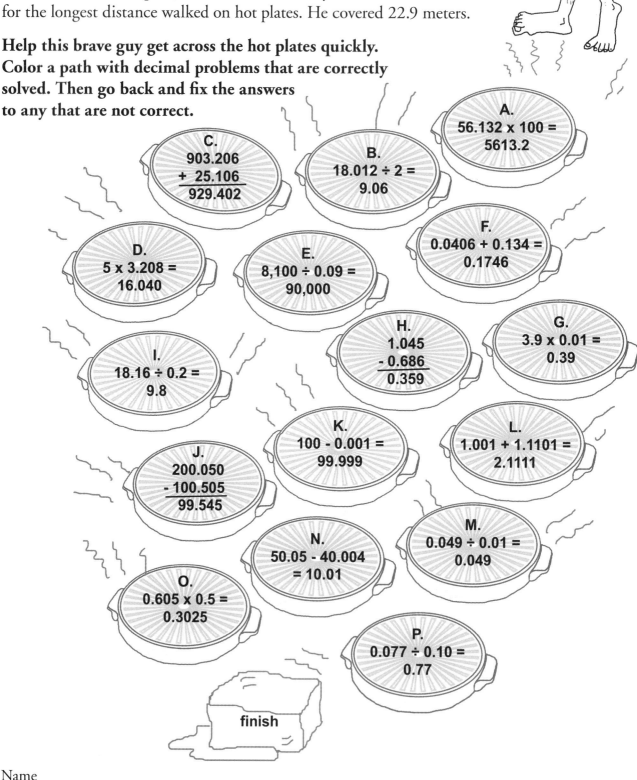

A.
56.132 x 100 =
5613.2

C.
903.206
+ 25.106
929.402

B.
18.012 ÷ 2 =
9.06

D.
5 x 3.208 =
16.040

E.
8,100 ÷ 0.09 =
90,000

F.
0.0406 + 0.134 =
0.1746

H.
1.045
- 0.686
0.359

G.
3.9 x 0.01 =
0.39

I.
18.16 ÷ 0.2 =
9.8

K.
100 - 0.001 =
99.999

L.
1.001 + 1.1101 =
2.1111

J.
200.050
- 100.505
99.545

M.
0.049 ÷ 0.01 =
0.049

N.
50.05 - 40.004
= 10.01

O.
0.605 x 0.5 =
0.3025

P.
0.077 ÷ 0.10 =
0.77

finish

Name

NUMBER
AND
OPERATIONS—
FRACTIONS

Grade 5

HIGH SPEEDS AND TOUGH TURNS

The Super Giant Slalom is said to take the most skill of any ski event. Skiers race down a mountain over a long, steep course at speeds of up to 80 miles per hour. They must go through a series of gates marked by flags.

For each problem, write an answer (in lowest terms) from one of the flags. Color the flag. The fraction will be in lowest terms.

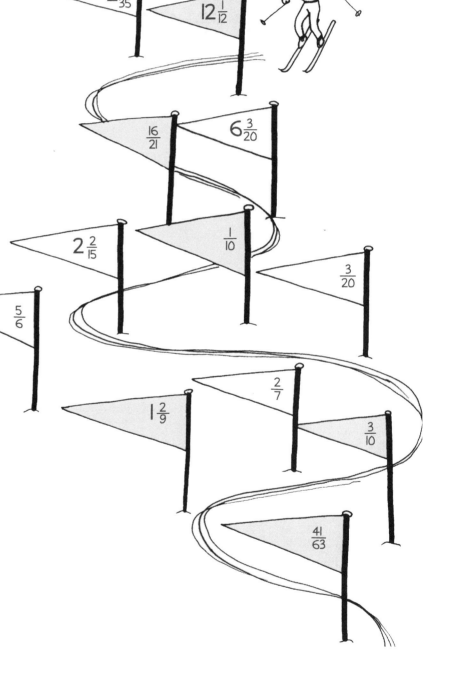

1. $\dfrac{1}{2} + \dfrac{1}{3} =$ _____

2. $\dfrac{2}{4} - \dfrac{1}{5} =$ _____

3. $\dfrac{3}{10} - \dfrac{1}{5} =$ _____

4. $\dfrac{5}{9} + \dfrac{2}{3} =$ _____

5. $\dfrac{15}{4} + \dfrac{24}{10} =$ _____

6. $\dfrac{3}{7} + \dfrac{2}{6} =$ _____

7. $2\dfrac{4}{5} - \dfrac{2}{3} =$ _____

8. $\dfrac{9}{5} + \dfrac{3}{7} =$ _____

9. $5\dfrac{3}{4} + 6\dfrac{1}{3} =$ _____

10. $\dfrac{9}{10} - \dfrac{3}{4} =$ _____

11. $\dfrac{2}{9} + \dfrac{3}{7} =$ _____

12. $\dfrac{18}{21} - \dfrac{4}{7} =$ _____

Name

THE #1 SPORT

Soccer is the most popular sport in the world. (In most places it is called *football*.) It was the first team sport to be included in the Olympics. At every Olympic Games, this sport draws some of the biggest crowds. In 1992, at the Barcelona, Spain Games, the mainly-Spanish crowd was thrilled to see their team win the gold medal!

Look on the soccer field below for the answer to each problem. Circle the correct answer with the color shown. Then write it on the line. Answers must be fractions in lowest terms.

Example: $\frac{1}{10} + \frac{1}{2} = \frac{1}{10} + \frac{5}{10} = \frac{6}{10}$ ($\frac{3}{5}$ *in lowest terms*)

1. ORANGE: $\frac{11}{12} - \frac{3}{4} =$ _____

2. PINK: $\frac{1}{2} + \frac{2}{22} =$ _____

3. BROWN: $\frac{10}{25} + \frac{2}{5} =$ _____

4. RED $\frac{20}{30} - \frac{2}{6} =$ _____

5. PURPLE: $\frac{1}{4} + \frac{4}{16} =$ _____

6. BLACK: $\frac{4}{7} + \frac{1}{3} =$ _____

7. YELLOW: $\frac{3}{4} - \frac{5}{8} =$ _____

8. BLUE: $\frac{5}{12} - \frac{1}{3} =$ _____

9. DARK GREEN: $\frac{2}{3} + \frac{1}{6} =$ _____

10. LIGHT GREEN: $\frac{5}{10} - \frac{1}{5} =$ _____

11. AQUA: $\frac{1}{6} + \frac{3}{4} - \frac{1}{8} =$ _____

12. GOLD: $\frac{11}{14} - \frac{3}{7} + \frac{1}{7} =$ _____

13. SILVER: $\frac{2}{9} + \frac{8}{9} - \frac{1}{3} =$ _____

14. LAVENDER: $\frac{1}{9} + \frac{2}{3} - \frac{1}{3} =$ _____

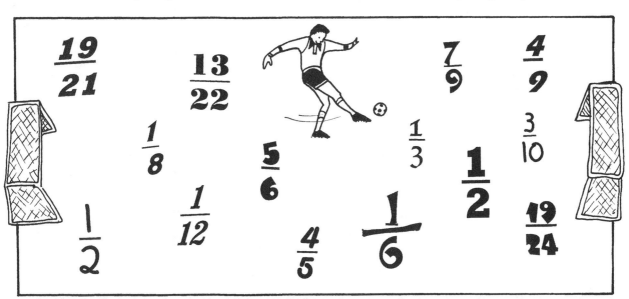

Name

LOST!

Badminton may look like an easy sport in which you just hit the "birdie" around at a slow pace. Actually, it is the world's fastest racket sport. The "birdies" are called *shuttlecocks*, and they travel as fast as 200 miles per hour!

To add or subtract fractions with unlike denominators, you must write one or more equivalent fractions to work with like denominators. Examine each problem. Is the number below it a common denominator for the two fractions? If so, color the square. The colored squares will create a path to help Pierre find his teammates.

$\frac{8}{12} + \frac{2}{3}$	$\frac{11}{6} - \frac{5}{3}$	$\frac{2}{5} + \frac{3}{4}$	$\frac{3}{4} - \frac{3}{6}$
12	21	10	18
$\frac{2}{4} - \frac{5}{10}$	$\frac{6}{3} + \frac{8}{4}$	$\frac{4}{5} - \frac{7}{10}$	$\frac{2}{9} + \frac{1}{2}$
20	12	25	27
$\frac{2}{5} + \frac{5}{10}$	$\frac{8}{4} + \frac{12}{6}$	$\frac{7}{6} + \frac{4}{3}$	$\frac{2}{3} - \frac{4}{6}$
45	12	7	6
$\frac{7}{16} - \frac{1}{4}$	$\frac{20}{25} + \frac{4}{5}$	$\frac{7}{12} + \frac{14}{24}$	$\frac{1}{2} - \frac{2}{5}$
8	25	12	10

Name

TRICKS GALORE

Wild Will has perfected a long list of snowboard tricks. Let's hope he can pull them off in this competition!

Read the tales about his practice and competition. Find the value of the missing number (n) to solve each problem.

1. I aced half of my tricks! On one-third, I did okay. I wiped out on the rest. On what fraction of the tricks did I wipe out?

   $1 - (\frac{1}{2} + \frac{1}{3}) = n$ **n =** _____

2. Over three weeks of practice, I ate 46 energy bars. The first week, I ate $16\frac{3}{4}$ bars. In the second week, I ate the same amount as during the first. How many bars did I eat in the third week?

   $(16\frac{3}{4} + 16\frac{3}{4}) + n = 46$ **n =** _____

3. During my practice, the Ollies took up $\frac{2}{5}$ of my time. The Fakies took up $\frac{2}{8}$ of my time. The rest of the time I practiced Tail Rolls. What fraction of my practice time was spent on Tail Rolls?

   $1 - (\frac{2}{5} + \frac{2}{8}) = n$ **n =** _____

4. On Monday, I got bruises over $\frac{1}{5}$ of my body. On Tuesday, I got new bruises over $\frac{1}{3}$ of the rest of my body. On Wednesday, I got bruises over $\frac{1}{4}$ of the remaining un-bruised body! How much of my body was left unbruised? Circle the equation that will help you find the answer. Then find the value of **n**.

   a. $1 - \frac{1}{5} - \frac{1}{3} - \frac{1}{4} = n$ **n =** _____

   b. $1 + \frac{1}{5} + \frac{1}{3} + \frac{1}{4} = n$ **n =** _____

   c. $1 \times (\frac{1}{5} + \frac{1}{3} + \frac{1}{5}) = n$ **n =** _____

   d. $n - \frac{1}{5} - \frac{1}{3} - \frac{1}{4} = 1$ **n =** _____

5. I spent $\frac{6}{10}$ of my money on passes to the ski hill, $\frac{1}{8}$ of my money on hot chocolate and snacks, and $\frac{1}{5}$ on wax for my board. What fraction of my money was left?

   $(\frac{6}{10} + \frac{1}{8} + \frac{1}{5}) + n = 1$ **n =** _____

Name _____

A SLIPPERY SLOPE

The climbing team is having some trouble this week. On an expedition to the top of Mount Slick, the climbers are finding the slopes to be very slippery. Each day they make progress upward, but on many steps they slide backward.

Look at the record of each climber's progress. Estimate the progress for each climber to decide if the final total is reasonable. Write *yes* or *no*.

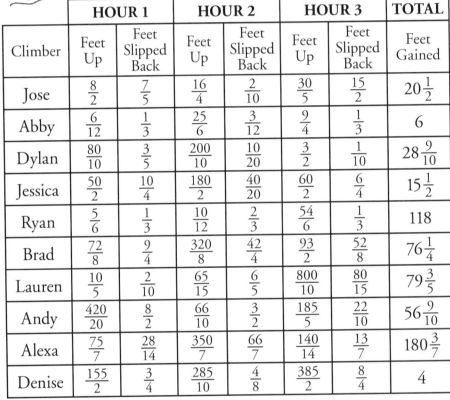

Climber	HOUR 1 Feet Up	HOUR 1 Feet Slipped Back	HOUR 2 Feet Up	HOUR 2 Feet Slipped Back	HOUR 3 Feet Up	HOUR 3 Feet Slipped Back	TOTAL Feet Gained
Jose	$\frac{8}{2}$	$\frac{7}{5}$	$\frac{16}{4}$	$\frac{2}{10}$	$\frac{30}{5}$	$\frac{15}{2}$	$20\frac{1}{2}$
Abby	$\frac{6}{12}$	$\frac{1}{3}$	$\frac{25}{6}$	$\frac{3}{12}$	$\frac{9}{4}$	$\frac{1}{3}$	6
Dylan	$\frac{80}{10}$	$\frac{3}{5}$	$\frac{200}{10}$	$\frac{10}{20}$	$\frac{3}{2}$	$\frac{1}{10}$	$28\frac{9}{10}$
Jessica	$\frac{50}{2}$	$\frac{10}{4}$	$\frac{180}{2}$	$\frac{40}{20}$	$\frac{60}{2}$	$\frac{6}{4}$	$15\frac{1}{2}$
Ryan	$\frac{5}{6}$	$\frac{1}{3}$	$\frac{10}{12}$	$\frac{2}{3}$	$\frac{54}{6}$	$\frac{1}{3}$	118
Brad	$\frac{72}{8}$	$\frac{9}{4}$	$\frac{320}{8}$	$\frac{42}{4}$	$\frac{93}{2}$	$\frac{52}{8}$	$76\frac{1}{4}$
Lauren	$\frac{10}{5}$	$\frac{2}{10}$	$\frac{65}{15}$	$\frac{6}{5}$	$\frac{800}{10}$	$\frac{80}{15}$	$79\frac{3}{5}$
Andy	$\frac{420}{20}$	$\frac{8}{2}$	$\frac{66}{10}$	$\frac{3}{2}$	$\frac{185}{5}$	$\frac{22}{10}$	$56\frac{9}{10}$
Alexa	$\frac{75}{7}$	$\frac{28}{14}$	$\frac{350}{7}$	$\frac{66}{7}$	$\frac{140}{14}$	$\frac{13}{7}$	$180\frac{3}{7}$
Denise	$\frac{155}{2}$	$\frac{3}{4}$	$\frac{285}{10}$	$\frac{4}{8}$	$\frac{385}{2}$	$\frac{8}{4}$	4

Choose two of the climbers for which you decided the answer given was NOT reasonable. Explain why.

1. Climber _____ Explanation: _____

_____

_____

2. Climber _____ Explanation: _____

_____

_____

Name _____

JUST HANGING AROUND

Gymnasts hang around the gym for hours. Male gymnasts also spend plenty of time hanging on rings. They practice skills in ways that they and their coaches decide are reasonable.

Write an equation to represent each problem. Then use estimation to help you decide if the calculation in the problem is reasonable. Write *yes* or *no* and explain your decision.

yes or *no*

_____ 1. The rings are suspended $95\frac{3}{4}$ inches from the floor. Jason asks to have them raised $3\frac{7}{12}$ inches to 98 inches. Has he calculated correctly?

Equation: _____

Explanation: _____

_____

_____ 2. Gymnasts are lined up at the drinking fountain. The first four each take $10\frac{3}{10}$ seconds. The fifth takes $5\frac{4}{5}$ seconds. The sixth and seventh each take $12\frac{2}{5}$ seconds. Mariah, who is eighth, calculates that she has waited 1 minute, $11\frac{4}{5}$ seconds for her turn. Is she right?

Equation: _____

Explanation: _____

_____

_____ 3. When Lorenzo does his floor routine, his first series of flips covers $10\frac{15}{100}$ meters of the 12-meter mat width. Has he left $1\frac{17}{20}$ meters uncovered?

Equation: _____

Explanation: _____

_____ 4. The spectators' bleachers measure $58\frac{1}{2}$ feet in length. All but $27\frac{5}{9}$ feet of the first two rows are saved for team members and families. Does this give a total of $30\frac{7}{18}$ feet of space for team members and families?

Equation: _____

Explanation: _____

Name _____

SINK THAT BASKET

The Panthers and Tigers are big rivals. This game will decide the league championship.

Circle the correct solution.

1. In the first half of the game, the Tigers scored 37 points.
   Eight different players played in the first half.
   What was the average number of points per player?

   a. 296　　　　　　b. $\frac{8}{37}$　　　　　　c. $\frac{37}{8}$ (or $4\frac{5}{8}$)

2. The Panthers traveled a total of 836 miles to their
   nine away games last season. What was the average
   number of miles traveled per game?

   a. $\frac{9}{836}$　　　　　b. 7,524　　　　　c. $\frac{836}{9}$ (or $92\frac{8}{9}$)

3. During the first quarter, 22 Panthers players shared
   12 gallons of water. Each player drank the same amount.
   What was the amount?

   a. 264 gal　　　　b. $\frac{12}{22}$ (or $\frac{6}{11}$) gal　　　c. $\frac{22}{12}$ gal (or $2\frac{5}{6}$)

4. Player Shaundra Perez dribbled the basketball a total distance
   of 800 meters during the game. She had the ball in her possession
   35 times. On average, how many meters did she dribble during
   each possession?

   a. $\frac{800}{35}$ (or $20\frac{5}{7}$)　　b. $\frac{35}{800}$ (or $\frac{7}{160}$)　　c. 28,000

5. Eight band members shared six bags of popcorn
   during the game. Each ate equal amounts.
   What part of a bag did each band member eat?

   a. $\frac{6}{8}$ (or $\frac{3}{4}$)　　　　b. $\frac{8}{6}$ (or $1\frac{1}{3}$)　　　　c. $\frac{48}{100}$

6. At the end of the game, all 20 players shared
   a huge bowl of pasta. That bowl contained 15 pounds
   of pasta, and each player was served the same amount.
   What was the weight of each serving?

   a. $\frac{20}{15}$ (or $1\frac{1}{4}$) lb　　b. $\frac{15}{20}$ (or $\frac{3}{4}$) lb　　c. 30 lb

Name

SUBMERGED SOLUTIONS

Use what you know about operations with fractions to examine these underwater solutions.

Explain how you can tell if each solution is correct.

1. When a reef shark headed for Samantha, she swam the 30 meters to the boat in 16 seconds. How long did it take to swim each meter?

   $\frac{16}{30}$ (or $\frac{8}{15}$) seconds

   Explanation: _____

   _____

   _____

2. Five divers found three chests of coins. They decided to divide the treasure evenly. What portion of a chest would each one get?

   $\frac{5}{3}$ of a chest

   Explanation: _____

   _____

   _____

3. Samantha and Sasha paid $99 for six dives. How much did each dive cost?

   $\frac{99}{6}$ or $16\frac{3}{6}$ or $16\frac{1}{2}$ or $16.50

   Explanation: _____

   _____

   _____

4. After a great dive, 12 divers equally shared 9 freshly-speared and freshly-cooked fish. How much did each diver get?

   $\frac{12}{9}$ or $1\frac{3}{9}$ or $1\frac{1}{3}$ fish

   Explanation: _____

   _____

   _____

Name

HITTING THE BRICKS

When you try to break a brick with your hand (or head), you have to hit it just right. Don't use the wrong approach, speed, angle, or technique!

Circle just the right fraction to answer each question.

SUNDAY

Eight bricks of equal weight
Total weight of all is 6 pounds
Weight per brick?

$\frac{8}{6}$ **lb** $\frac{6}{8}$ **lb**

MONDAY

Karate teacher works 9 hours
Time divided among seven pupils
Time per pupil?

$\frac{7}{9}$ **hr** $\frac{9}{7}$ **hr**

THURSDAY

7 hours of music
15 pupils each contribute equal amount
How much time per pupil?

$\frac{7}{15}$ **hr** $\frac{15}{7}$ **hr**

TUESDAY

12 liters of water
15 competitors drinking equal amounts
Amount per competitor?

$\frac{15}{12}$ **l** $\frac{12}{15}$ **l**

FRIDAY

50 pounds of bricks for practice
Equal amounts for each of 16 pupils
Amount per pupil?

$\frac{16}{50}$ **lb** $\frac{50}{16}$ **lb**

WEDNESDAY

Prize money $40
Divided among 6 winners
Amount per winner?

$\frac{40}{6}$ $\frac{6}{40}$

SATURDAY

10 bowls of fried rice
14 hungry competitors sharing equally
Amount of rice per competitor?

$\frac{10}{14}$ **bowl** $\frac{14}{10}$ **bowl**

Name

WEIGHTY PROBLEMS

Every time the weightlifter adds weights to the bar, his work is multiplied! Use your fraction multiplication skills to solve these "weighty" problems.

Circle the correct value of *n* for each problem.

1. Before a training session, Kino drinks $1\frac{5}{8}$ liters of energy drink. He has 9 training sessions a week. How many liters will he drink?

    $1\frac{5}{8}$ x 9 = n

    a. $n = \frac{13}{72}$ b. $n = \frac{8}{117}$ c. $n = \frac{72}{13}$ d. $14\frac{5}{8}$

2. To stay in his weight class, Jamal has been gaining $\frac{6}{4}$ pounds a week. At this rate, how many pounds will he gain in 15 weeks?

    15 x $\frac{6}{4}$ = n

    a. $n = 22\frac{1}{2}$ b. $n = 15$ c. $n = \frac{40}{9}$ d. $n = \frac{6}{60}$

3. Juliette jogs $\frac{16}{10}$ mile to the gym each day for her training session. Lucinda jogs $\frac{4}{5}$ of that distance to the gym. How many miles does Lucinda jog each day?

    $n = \frac{4}{5}$ x $\frac{16}{10}$

    a. $n = \frac{40}{80}$ b. $n = \frac{64}{50}$ c. $n = \frac{20}{64}$ d. $n = 2$

4. Each time Bruno takes a shower, he uses $20\frac{3}{4}$ gallons of water. How much water is used in 10 showers?

    $20\frac{3}{4}$ x 10 = n

    a. $n = \frac{203}{4}$ b. $n = 200\frac{3}{4}$ c. $n = 207\frac{1}{2}$ d. $n = \frac{83}{40}$

5. Misha has a bag with 12 energy bars. Each one weighs $4\frac{1}{2}$ ounces. She shares $\frac{4}{6}$ of the total amount with Amos. How many ounces does she give away?

    $(12 \times 4\frac{1}{2})$ x $\frac{4}{6}$ = n

    a. $n = \frac{108}{2}$ b. $n = 36$ c. $n = \frac{8}{648}$ d. $n = \frac{16}{12}$

6. When Zeke walked into the lounge, Marcos had $\frac{8}{16}$ of a pizza left. He shared $\frac{5}{12}$ of that with Zeke. How much of the pizza did Zeke get?

    $\frac{5}{12}$ x $\frac{8}{16}$ = n

    a. $n = \frac{192}{40}$ b. $n = \frac{24}{5}$ c. $n = \frac{5}{24}$ d. $n = \frac{40}{16}$

Name _____

HITTING THEIR STRIDE

To skate their fastest time, speed skaters need to "hit their stride." This means they need to get their steps (strides) moving in the right rhythm that keeps them moving fast.

Help the skaters hit their stride by solving the problems. Find and write the product. Color the matching section of the skating track.

1. Practice sessions: 8
   Time: $\frac{4}{9}$ hr each   Total time? _____

2. Speed: 27 m per min
   Time: $\frac{1}{3}$ min.   Distance? _____

3. Practice sessions: 10
   Time: $\frac{5}{9}$ hr each   Total time? _____

4. Speed: $\frac{4}{3}$ yd per sec
   Time: 2 sec.   Distance? _____

5. Practice sessions: 7
   Time: $\frac{1}{3}$ hr each   Total time? _____

6. Speed: 4 m per min
   Time: $\frac{9}{5}$ min   Distance? _____

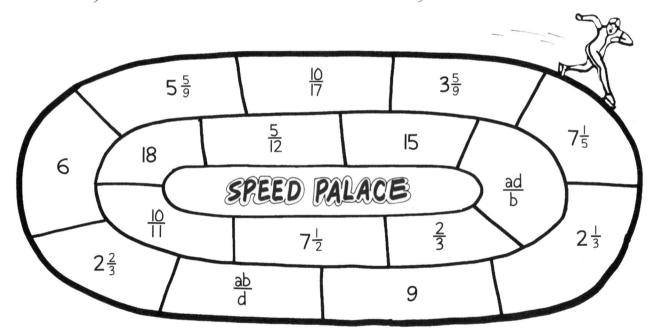

7. Laps: $\frac{5}{3}$ laps per min   Time: 9 min   Total laps? _____

8. 3 skaters   Pasta per skater: $\frac{5}{2}$ lb   Total pasta eaten? _____

9. Laps: $\frac{a}{b}$ laps per min   Time: d min   Total laps? _____

10. 8 skaters   Pasta per skater: $\frac{12}{16}$ lb   Total pasta eaten? _____

11. Laps: $\frac{2}{11}$ laps per min   Time: 5 min   Total laps? _____

12. 9 skaters   Pasta per skater: $\frac{8}{4}$ lb   Total pasta eaten? _____

Name _____

BE CAREFUL NOT TO SWING

A male gymnast does some difficult moves while he hangs from rings. Gymnasts show amazing skill and strength as they hold their bodies in hard positions. The rings are not supposed to swing or wobble. The gymnast's body and arms are not supposed to wobble, sag, or shake.

Keep these rings from wobbling by matching a number from the ring to each equation. Color the ring as you use a fraction.

1. $\left(\frac{a}{b}\right) \times g$ = _____

2. $\frac{5}{2} \times \frac{6}{3}$ = _____

3. $\frac{1}{2} \times \frac{3}{4}$ = _____

4. $\frac{5}{7} \times \frac{2}{4}$ = _____

5. $\frac{5}{8} \times \frac{2}{10}$ = _____

6. $\left(\frac{a}{g}\right) \times b$ = _____

7. $\frac{2}{3} \times \frac{7}{9}$ = _____

8. $\frac{3}{10} \times \frac{3}{2}$ = _____

9. $\frac{4}{5} \times \frac{7}{2}$ = _____

10. $\frac{8}{6} \times \frac{3}{5}$ = _____

11. $\frac{6}{10} \times \frac{8}{4}$ = _____

12. $\frac{2}{4} \times \frac{15}{6}$ = _____

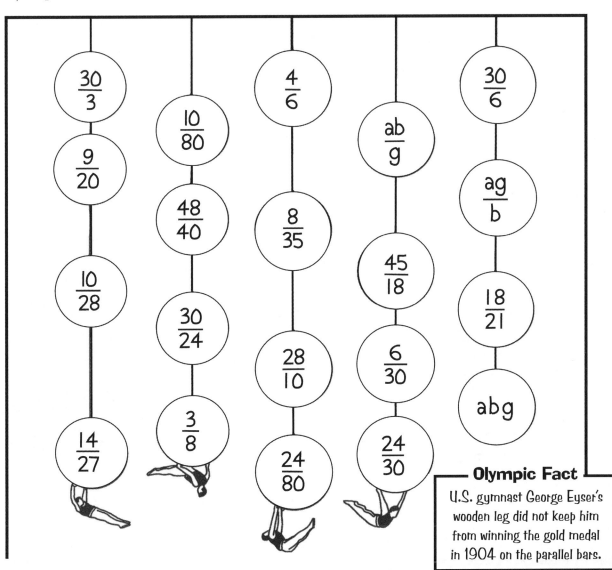

Olympic Fact

U.S. gymnast George Eyser's wooden leg did not keep him from winning the gold medal in 1904 on the parallel bars.

Name

Common Core Reinforcement Activities — 5th Grade Math

GREAT COVERAGE

Athletes cover a lot of distance playing, running, hitting or throwing or kicking balls, swimming, wrestling, boxing, or leaping on different surfaces. These surfaces—fields, courts, pools, or mats—cover areas of different sizes.

Figure out the area available to athletes for playing their games on the rectangular surfaces on this page and page 73. Write the area inside each figure.

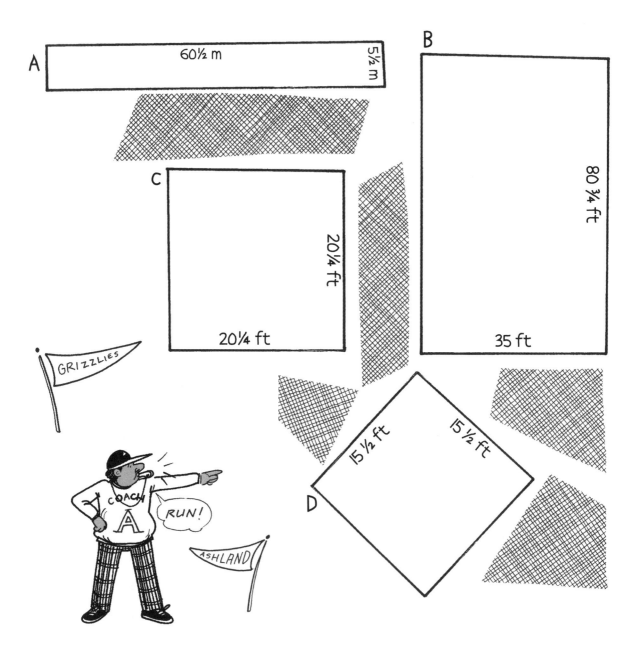

Use with page 73.

Name

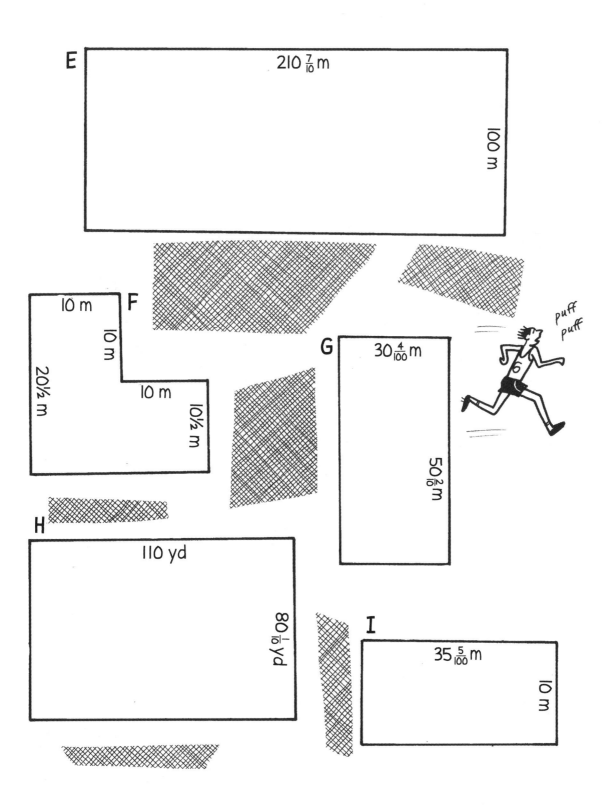

E $210\frac{7}{10}$ m

100 m

F 10 m

10 m

$20\frac{1}{2}$ m

10 m

$10\frac{1}{2}$ m

G $30\frac{4}{100}$ m

$50\frac{2}{10}$ m

puff puff

H 110 yd

$80\frac{1}{10}$ yd

I $35\frac{5}{100}$ m

10 m

Use with page 72.

Name

©Incentive Publications, Inc., Nashville, TN

Common Core Reinforcement Activities — 5th Grade Math

GETTING TO VENUES

Olympic events are held in locations called *venues*. Spectators arrive to watch the events. But the athletes have to get there too!

These athletes are heading for venues but their paths are blocked. Remove obstacles by finding the solutions.

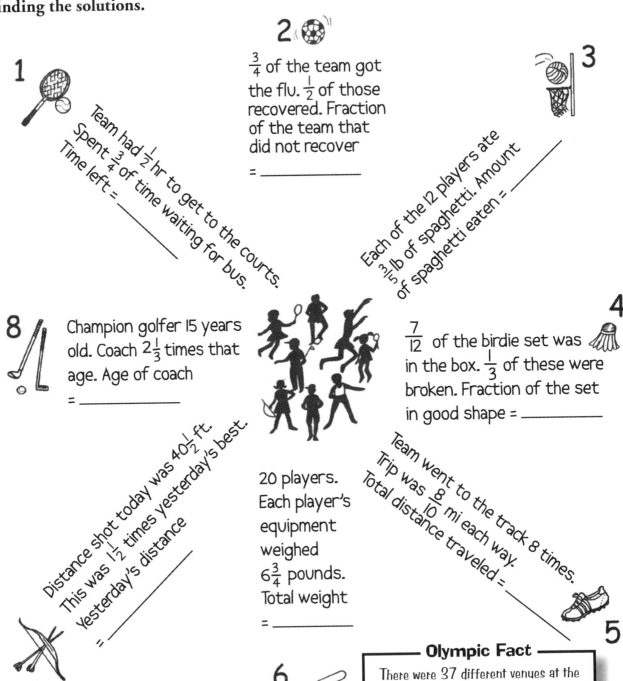

1

Team had $\frac{1}{2}$ hr to get to the courts. Spent $\frac{3}{4}$ of time waiting for bus. Time left = _____

2

$\frac{3}{4}$ of the team got the flu. $\frac{1}{2}$ of those recovered. Fraction of the team that did not recover

= _____

3

Each of the 12 players ate $\frac{3}{5}$ lb of spaghetti. Amount of spaghetti eaten = _____

4

$\frac{7}{12}$ of the birdie set was in the box. $\frac{1}{3}$ of these were broken. Fraction of the set in good shape = _____

5

Team went to the track 8 times. Trip was $\frac{8}{10}$ mi each way. Total distance traveled = _____

6

20 players. Each player's equipment weighed $6\frac{3}{4}$ pounds. Total weight

= _____

7

Distance shot today was $40\frac{1}{2}$ ft. This was $1\frac{1}{2}$ times yesterday's best. Yesterday's distance

= _____

8

Champion golfer 15 years old. Coach $2\frac{1}{3}$ times that age. Age of coach

= _____

Olympic Fact

There were 37 different venues at the 2012 Olympic Games in London. The sailing races took place 125 miles away, around the Isle of Portland.

EN GARDE!

Fencing was an event at the first Modern Olympic Games in 1986. It is an old sport that began around 400 B. C. Fencers use different kinds of swords: the foil, the épée, and the sabre. When the bout director calls "en garde," the competitors take a ready position. They begin the bout when the director gives the command: "fence."

Try your skill with this bout of multiplication questions.

2.
How will the product of 150 x 150 compare to the product of 150 x 25? (Explain why.)

3.
Is this statement true? The product of $\frac{3}{4}$ x 12 is greater than the product of $\frac{5}{6}$ x 12. Discuss your answer.

1.
Fencing bouts take place on a dueling surface called a *piste* or *fencing strip*. The strip is 14 meters long and 2 meters wide. Lucas practices on a strip the same length but half as wide. How would the area of his strip compare to the usual strip area? (Explain why.)

4.
Tonya's fencing bout lasted 9 minutes. Shura's lasted $\frac{3}{5}$ that long. Angela's lasted $\frac{1}{2}$ as long as Tonya's. How will the length of Shura's bout compare to the length of Tonya's?

épée = 770 grams

foil = 500 grams

Sabre = 500 grams

6.
How will the product of 88 x 40 compare to the product of 60 x 88? (Explain why.)

5.
Is this statement true? The product of 12 x 60 is $\frac{3}{4}$ the product of 16 x 60. Discuss your answer.

Olympic Fact

Fencers began to wear white uniforms because ink from the end of the weapon would leave a spot when a hit was made. The ink showed up well on the white. This practice is no longer followed, but fencers still wear the white uniforms. Some fencers would dip their uniforms in vinegar so the mark would not show.

Name

OVER THE HURDLES

The Olympic hurdle event is a fast sprinting race with a series of barriers to jump. The hurdles are mostly made of metal, and sometimes runners knock them over as they jump. It doesn't disqualify a hurdler to knock one over, but usually it slows him or her down a little. Men and women compete in hurdle events of different lengths and with different height hurdles.

Help this runner clear her hurdles by answering these questions about multiplication of fractions. For each one, decide if the product will be greater than the first factor. Circle *yes* or *no*. Then explain how you know.

— Olympic Fact —

In 1988, hurdler Gail Devers faced the biggest hurdle of her life. Due to Grave's disease, she could not walk. Doctors thought they would have to amputate her feet. Instead, she came back to win gold medals in the 100-meter sprint at the 1992 and 1996 Olympics.

1. $15 \times \frac{9}{10}$ *yes*   *no*

    How do you know? _____

    _____

    _____

2. $100 \times \frac{9}{8}$ *yes*   *no*

    How do you know? _____

    _____

    _____

3. $65 \times 3\frac{1}{2}$ *yes*   *no*

    How do you know? _____

    _____

    _____

4. $21 \times \frac{6}{4}$ *yes*   *no*

    How do you know? _____

    _____

    _____

5. $33 \times \frac{7}{9}$ *yes*   *no*

    How do you know? _____

    _____

    _____

6. $175 \times \frac{3}{4}$ *yes*   *no*

    How do you know? _____

    _____

    _____

7. $72 \times 2\frac{3}{4}$ *yes*   *no*

    How do you know? _____

    _____

    _____

8. $49 \times \frac{9}{7}$ *yes*   *no*

    How do you know? _____

    _____

    _____

Name _____

THROUGH WILD WATERS

In the Olympic kayaking events, kayakers race through wild, foaming water (known as whitewater). They must get down the river through a series of gates safely and speedily. Some of the gates require them to paddle upstream against the raging waters! Of course, sometimes the kayaks flip, but the athletes are good at turning right side up again.

Help the kayaker through the whitewater by answering these questions about multiplication of fractions.

Examine each problem. Decide if the product will be less than, greater than, or equal to the first factor. (Circle one.) Then explain your answer.

1. $\frac{1}{2}$ x $\frac{5}{6}$ **<**   **>**   **=**

   How do you know? _____

   _____

   _____

2. $\frac{6}{8}$ x $\frac{7}{7}$ **<**   **>**   **=**

   How do you know? _____

   _____

   _____

3. $\frac{9}{12}$ x $\frac{8}{6}$ **<**   **>**   **=**

   How do you know? _____

   _____

   _____

4. $\frac{4}{9}$ x $3\frac{2}{5}$ **<**   **>**   **=**

   How do you know? _____

   _____

   _____

5. $5\frac{1}{3}$ x $\frac{7}{8}$ **<**   **>**   **=**

   How do you know? _____

   _____

   _____

Think about how the product will compare to the factors.

6. $7\frac{1}{2}$ x 3

   Product will fall between these numbers:

   It will be > _____ and < _____.

   How do you know? _____

   _____

   _____

   _____

7. $2\frac{2}{3}$ x 24

   Product will fall between these numbers:

   It will be > _____ and < _____.

   How do you know? _____

   _____

   _____

Name _____

BRUNO'S BREW

Big Bruno makes energy shakes for all his weight-lifting friends. One batch makes enough for four weightlifters. Pay close attention to the recipe as you solve the problems.

Write an equation to solve each problem. Find a solution.

3½ cups milk
6 raw eggs
3¼ bananas
¾ teaspoon vanilla
⅔ cup of protein powder

1. By mistake, Bruno put in $2\frac{1}{2}$ times the amount of vanilla. How much vanilla was in the shake?

2. Bruno decided to multiply the amount of protein powder by 4 times. How much powder did he put in?

3. For fun, he doubled the number of bananas. What was the new amount of bananas?

4. Bruno shared $\frac{1}{5}$ of the total shake with a friend. How much milk would be in $\frac{1}{5}$ of this shake?

5. In the next shake, Bruno decides he will use $\frac{1}{2}$ the amount of bananas. How many bananas will be in the next shake?

6. Bruno tripled the recipe to serve 12 friends. How much milk will he need?

Name

TICKET MANIA

The ticket line for the big game has been growing. Everyone is lining up early, because the word is that the game will be sold out! Solve these problems about the fans and their purchases.

Write an equation that can be used to solve the problem. (Write two equations, if needed.) Use *n* for the unknown number. Then solve the equation for *n*.

1. Jackson waited in line for $\frac{4}{5}$ hour. Lucinda waited $\frac{2}{3}$ as long as Jackson. How long (in minutes) did Lucinda wait?

2. Carlos brought along $8\frac{3}{9}$-ounces of popcorn for the game. He ate $\frac{1}{4}$ of it while he waited in line. How much popcorn was left for the game?

3. Mrs. Gehman bought 8 adult tickets and 5 tickets for children. The main ticket price was $6\frac{1}{2}$ dollars. Children's tickets were half price. How much did Mrs. Gehman spend?

4. Destiny waited $\frac{9}{12}$ of an hour. Her brother Eli joined her for the last $\frac{3}{4}$ of that time. How long (in minutes) did Eli wait in line?

5. While she waited in line, Destiny made several phone calls. She was on the phone $\frac{4}{9}$ of the time she was in line. She talked to the lady in front of her $\frac{1}{4}$ as long as she spent on the phone. What fraction of her time in line was spent talking to the lady in front of her?

6. Mr. Bryson carried a baby who weighed $15\frac{3}{4}$ pounds. The girl behind him, Riley, carried a bag that weighed $\frac{2}{7}$ as much. How much did Riley's bag weigh?

Name _____

HOT OLYMPIC STEW

Sixty cold, hungry skiers planned to stop at the ski lodge to warm up with some hearty Olympic Stew. The cook's recipe was intended to serve twenty-four, so she knew she'd have to double the recipe to have enough.

Rewrite the stew recipe to feed 60. To do this, you will need to multiply all ingredients by $2\frac{1}{2}$. Write all amounts in lowest terms. Use a separate piece of paper to find the new amounts.

Olympic Stew for 24

$5\frac{1}{2}$ pounds potatoes

$8\frac{1}{4}$ quarts boiling water

2 large onions

$8\frac{1}{8}$ cups chicken broth

$4\frac{2}{3}$ carrots, chopped

$8\frac{1}{2}$ celery sticks, sliced

$1\frac{1}{2}$ green peppers, chopped

$5\frac{1}{3}$ cups frozen corn

$4\frac{3}{4}$ pounds mushrooms

$7\frac{1}{4}$ cups cooked chicken, diced

$3\frac{1}{3}$ teaspoons salt

$6\frac{1}{3}$ Tablespoons mixed herbs

Mix all ingredients in a large pot. Cook over medium heat for one hour, stirring often.

Olympic Stew for 60

_____

_____

_____

_____

_____

_____

_____

_____

_____

_____

_____

_____

_____

_____

_____

_____

_____

_____

Name

LOCKER ROOM MYSTERIES

Coach Crunch has spent the day unlocking some mysteries in the locker room. There are strange smells and sounds coming from some lockers. As she opens the lockers, help her figure out just what is in those lockers!

Solve each equation to find the value of *n*.

1. Cass's locker contains $3\frac{1}{3}$ pounds of stinky, melted Gorgonzola cheese. Lucinda's locker has even more cheese! She's got $4\frac{1}{2}$ times the amount. How much cheese is in Lucinda's locker?

   $n = 4\frac{1}{2} \times 3\frac{1}{3}$ n = _____ pounds

2. There were terrible sounds in Locker 46. There was something strange sticking out of Locker 35. It took Coach $3\frac{4}{5}$ minutes to get into Locker 46. It took $\frac{5}{6}$ of that time to get into Locker 35. How long did it take to get into Locker 35?

   $n = \frac{5}{6} \times 3\frac{4}{5}$ n = _____ minutes

3. It took $12\frac{3}{4}$ ounces of soap powder to wash the sweaty socks found in Lockers 51, 56, and 61. It took $5\frac{1}{3}$ times that much soap to scrub out all the lockers. How much soap was needed for the locker-scrubbing job?

   $n = 5\frac{1}{3} \times 12\frac{3}{4}$ n = _____ ounces

4. Coach required all the girls to take part in the locker cleanup. The girls who had cheese in their lockers spent $1\frac{2}{3}$ hours cleaning. The rest of the girls spent $\frac{4}{10}$ that time cleaning. How long (in minutes) did the second group of girls clean?

   $n = \frac{4}{10} \times 1\frac{2}{3} \times 60$ n = _____ minutes

Name _____

HANG THOSE TOES!

The surf's up at Shark Beach! One hundred surfers showed up on Saturday to "hang ten" for the awesome waves. Hanging ten is a special stunt where the surfer positions the board so that the wave is at the back of the board and he or she can hang all ten toes over the nose of the surfboard.

Use the rectangle to create a visual model of the problem. Choose a fraction from the wave that solves the problem.

1. $\frac{1}{5} \div 2 =$

2. $\frac{3}{7} \div 2 =$

3. $\frac{2}{3} \div 4 =$

4. $\frac{4}{5} \div 3 =$

5. $\frac{1}{2} \div 6 =$

6. $\frac{3}{4} \div 4 =$

7. $\frac{1}{2} \div 3 =$

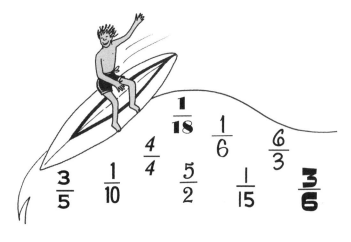

$\frac{1}{18}$ $\frac{1}{6}$ $\frac{6}{3}$

$\frac{4}{4}$

$\frac{3}{5}$ $\frac{1}{10}$ $\frac{5}{2}$ $\frac{1}{15}$ $\frac{3}{6}$

8. $\frac{4}{5} \div 4 =$

Name

FANTASTIC FINISHES

The race is on! Division is needed to solve the problems.

Think about what the answer to each question will be. Circle the correct choice.

1. The front runner has completed $\frac{7}{8}$ of the race distance. This is twice the amount completed by the person in last place (not shown in the picture). How much of the race has the last-place runner completed?

   a. $\frac{14}{16}$ b. $\frac{7}{16}$ c. $\frac{14}{8}$

2. Mason had a fantastic finish in the race pictured, with a time of $\frac{46}{10}$ minutes. But he was even happier with his next race, where he finished in half the time. What was the time for his next race?

   a. $2\frac{3}{10}$ min   b. $4\frac{3}{5}$ min   c. $9\frac{1}{5}$ min

3. Before the race, Michael stretched for $6\frac{1}{2}$ minutes. This time was three times as long as Alex stretched. How long did Alex stretch?

   a. $\frac{6}{13}$ min   b. $2\frac{1}{6}$ min   c. 13 min

4. After the race, Diego shared $\frac{8}{12}$ gallon of orange juice equally with 3 other runners. How much did each runner drink?

   a. $\frac{2}{9}$ gal   b. $4\frac{1}{2}$ gal   c. 2 gal

5. Julius ran the race in $5\frac{7}{8}$ minutes. The race course had three different sections: one grassy, one gravel-covered, and one through mud. If he ran at a steady rate, how long did it take him to cover the muddy part of the course?

   a. $\frac{24}{47}$ b. $17\frac{5}{8}$ c. $1\frac{23}{24}$

6. Cole walked to cool down for $\frac{1}{6}$ the time that Hunter walked. This is four times the distance that Aaron walked to cool down. What fraction of Hunter's cool-down time did Aaron walk? (The graph below is a model of this problem.)

   a. $\frac{1}{6}$ b. $\frac{4}{24}$ c. $\frac{1}{24}$

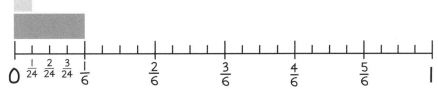

Name

OVER THE TOP

Pole vaulters sprint along a short track with a long pole that bends easily. Then they plant the pole into sand and soar upside down over a bar that might be as high as 20 feet. The goal is to make it over the top without knocking off that bar!

Answer the questions *yes* or *no*. Tell how you decided your answer.

1. Is 5 divided by $\frac{1}{3}$ equal to 15? _____
   How do you know? _____
   _____

2. Is 4 divided by $\frac{1}{6}$ equal to $\frac{2}{3}$? _____
   How do you know? _____
   _____

3. Is 20 divided by $\frac{1}{5}$ equal to 4? _____
   How do you know? _____
   _____

4. Is 7 divided by $\frac{1}{2}$ equal to 14? _____
   How do you know? _____
   _____

5. Is 9 divided by $\frac{1}{4}$ equal to $\frac{4}{36}$? _____
   How do you know? _____
   _____

6. Is 15 divided by $\frac{1}{6}$ equal to $2\frac{1}{2}$? _____
   How do you know? _____

Use the diagram below to answer #7.

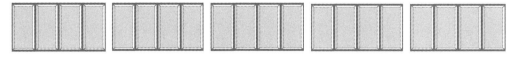

7. What problem is represented by the diagram? _____
   _____

Name _____

PENTATHLON QUESTIONS

Penta means *five*, and athlon means *competition*. So athletes who compete in the pentathlon must be good at five different sports. The modern pentathlon includes five events: pistol shooting, fencing, 200 m freestyle swimming, show jumping, and a 3 km cross-country run.

Show your skill in the following five fraction "events." Answer the question and explain how you arrived at your answer.

1. Swimming: How many $\frac{1}{2}$-liter portions of water are in a full 2 million-liter swimming pool? _____

   Explain: _____

   _____

2. Riding: How many $\frac{2}{8}$-pound handfuls of hay are in a 40-pound bale of hay? _____

   Explain: _____

   _____

3. Shooting: How many $\frac{3}{10}$-kilogram pistol bullets are in a full 15-kilogram box of bullets? _____

   Explain: _____

   _____

4. Fencing: How many $6\frac{4}{5}$-ounce servings of pre-event Energy Juice are in a full 34-ounce cooler? _____

   Explain: _____

   _____

5. Running: How many $\frac{3}{9}$-mile laps are in a 15-mile race? _____

   Explain: _____

   _____

Name _____

BUMPS, BRUISES, AND BREAKS

Most sports have chances for injuries. In some sports, there are lots of injuries. Take a close look at some problems about the bumps, bruises, and breaks that can come along with the fun of a sport.

Look at the answers that different athletes have given for problems on this page and page 87. Are they correct? Circle *yes* or *no*. Explain each of your answers.

1. Three injured hockey players shared an ambulance to the hospital. The ambulance charged by the mile for the $8\frac{2}{3}$-mile trip. How many miles' cost would be charged to each player? *Answer: $2\frac{8}{9}$ miles*

   Is this correct?   **yes   no**

   Explain: _____

   _____

   _____

   _____

2. During a football game, there were plenty of crashes and falls. Players kept a big bottle of aspirin handy. The bottle held $\frac{40}{32}$ ounces of aspirin. Twenty players needed aspirin. If the bottle was shared equally, how many ounces would each get? *Answer: $\frac{2}{32}$ (or $\frac{1}{16}$) ounce*

   Is this correct?   **yes   no**

   Explain: _____

   _____

   _____

   _____

3. Five players had to leave a basketball game at different points due to bloody noses. In total, there were $10\frac{2}{5}$ minutes of the game when a player was out. If the time-outs were equal, for how many minutes was each player out? *Answer: $2\frac{1}{5}$ minutes*

   Is this correct?   **yes   no**

   Explain: _____

   _____

   _____

   _____

4. A few boxers had their broken jaws wired shut. In the hospital, they were served milkshakes from a full 50-quart jug. How many $\frac{4}{10}$-quart portions of milkshake can be served from that jug? *Answer: $\frac{4}{500}$ portions*

   Is this correct?   **yes   no**

   Explain: _____

   _____

   _____

   _____

Use with page 87.

Name

Divide Fractions, Real-World Problems

Look at the answers that team members have given for the injury problems on this page and page 86. Are they correct?

Circle *yes* or *no*. Explain each of your answers.

5. At the emergency room, nurses used $5\frac{1}{2}$ boxes of bandages to cover the cuts of 12 battered skiers. How much of the bandages were used for each skier? *Answer: $\frac{6}{24}$ or $\frac{1}{4}$ boxes*

   Is this correct?   **yes   no**

   Explain: _____

   _____

   _____

   _____

6. During one boxing match, the doctor spent a total of $\frac{5}{6}$ hour attending to five injured boxers. If his time was given equally, how much time was spent with each boxer? *Answer: $\frac{5}{30}$ or $\frac{1}{6}$ hour*

   Is this correct?   **yes   no**

   Explain: _____

   _____

   _____

   _____

7. The speed skating race tournament ended with 20 broken arms. The emergency room was short on material for making casts. They had 200 yards. Each cast takes about $4\frac{5}{6}$ yards. Does the hospital have enough for the skaters' broken arms? *Answer: no*

   Is this correct?   **yes   no**

   Explain: _____

   _____

   _____

   _____

8. The emergency room must keep many doses of painkiller medicine on hand. Tonight, they have one 8-ounce container left. How many $\frac{4}{10}$-ounce doses can they give? *Answer: 20 doses*

   Is this correct?   **yes   no**

   Explain: _____

   _____

   _____

   _____

Use with page 86.

Name _____

PRACTICE MAKES PERFECT

Athletes practice for hours. These hours add up to weeks, months, and even years.

Practice your fraction skills. Examine each problem. Draw a visual model to find and support a solution.

1. Makayla likes to divide her practice time (and rest time) into segments of $\frac{4}{6}$ hour. She has 4 hours to be at the gym today. How many segments can she complete? _____

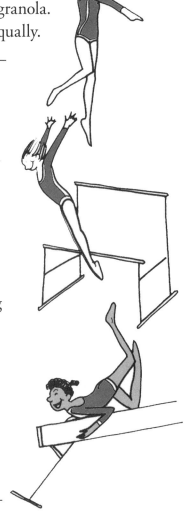

2. When Anna heads for the locker room, she gets out her bag of granola. She has $\frac{3}{5}$ of a bag full. She wants to share this with 4 friends equally. (Count Anna, too.) How much will each friend get? _____

3. When Anya's mom brings her to the gym, the car uses $\frac{3}{4}$ gallon of gas. The car's tank has 6 gallons left. How many more trips to the gym can she make before the tank is empty? _____

4. Leah spends $\frac{2}{3}$ of the money she has left on 3 hours of coaching time. What portion of her money does each hour of coaching take? _____

5. Sofia gives out all of the band-aids she has. Between herself and three friends, she uses up the remaining $\frac{2}{3}$ of the box. What portion of the box goes to each of the 4 girls? _____

Name _____

MEASUREMENT
AND
DATA

Grade 5

MEASUREMENT SENSE

It's time for new soccer uniforms. Olive's friend Maya is helping her take some measurements.

Consider whether Maya's and Olive's ideas about the measurements make sense. Answer each question.

_____ 1. Maya measured from Olive's shoulder to the tip of her finger. The distance was 20 centimeters. Maya says this was 200 meters. Is she right?

_____ 2. Olive measures her own head. She says the circumference is 6 inches. Is this reasonable?

_____ 3. Olive's soccer socks are 22 inches from top to toe. Maya thinks this is almost 2 feet in length. Is she right?

_____ 4. The soccer field at Olive's school is 110 meters long. She thinks this is the same as 1.1 kilometers. Is she right?

_____ 5. Yesterday's soccer game began at 2:45 p.m. It ended at 4:10 p.m. Olive told her mom the game lasted 75 minutes. Is she right?

_____ 6. The diameter of a soccer ball is 22 centimeters. Maya decides that this is 0.22 meters. Is she right?

_____ 7. Each of Olive's new soccer shoes weighs 9.7 ounces. She's sure that she is carrying around more than 3 pounds on her feet. Is this true?

_____ 8. At the end of the game, each of the 15 soccer players drank 1,000 milliliters of water. Olive calculated that this was 15 liters. Is she right?

_____ 9. When Maya puts all her soccer stuff in a bag, it weighs 2,100 grams. She thinks this weighs about 2 kilograms. Is she right?

_____ 10. The soccer game traveled 158 kilometers to the championship game. Olive says this is 158,000 meters. Maya says this is 15,800,000 centimeters. Who is right?

Name _____

MORE, LESS, OR EQUAL?

Ooops! The weightlifters have a problem at practice today. The weights on both ends of the bars are not equal for every athlete!

The measurements below have the same problem. Some of them are not equal on both sides. Compare them. Write > (greater than), < (less than), or = in each circle.

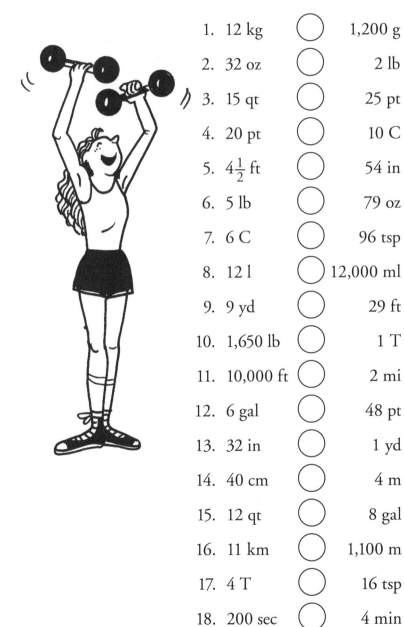

1. 12 kg $\bigcirc$ 1,200 g

2. 32 oz $\bigcirc$ 2 lb

3. 15 qt $\bigcirc$ 25 pt

4. 20 pt $\bigcirc$ 10 C

5. $4\frac{1}{2}$ ft $\bigcirc$ 54 in

6. 5 lb $\bigcirc$ 79 oz

7. 6 C $\bigcirc$ 96 tsp

8. 12 l $\bigcirc$ 12,000 ml

9. 9 yd $\bigcirc$ 29 ft

10. 1,650 lb $\bigcirc$ 1 T

11. 10,000 ft $\bigcirc$ 2 mi

12. 6 gal $\bigcirc$ 48 pt

13. 32 in $\bigcirc$ 1 yd

14. 40 cm $\bigcirc$ 4 m

15. 12 qt $\bigcirc$ 8 gal

16. 11 km $\bigcirc$ 1,100 m

17. 4 T $\bigcirc$ 16 tsp

18. 200 sec $\bigcirc$ 4 min

19. 9 hr $\bigcirc$ 540 min

20. 15 gal $\bigcirc$ 60 pt

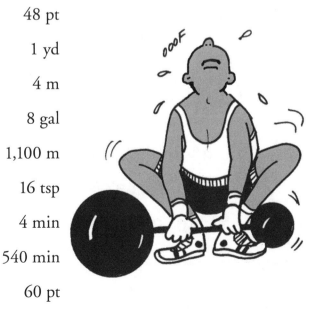

Name _____

91 *Common Core Reinforcement Activities — 5th Grade Math*

PASSING THE TEST

In most schools, athletes must keep good grades in order to play a school sport. How is Ted doing on his measurement test? He needs to have 9 correct in order to pass the test.

Circle the numbers of the correct answers. Cross out the wrong answers, and replace them with the correct answers.

Measurement Test

Student Name: **Ted**   Date: **January 6**

1. Length can be measured in _kilograms_ .
2. Would 5 milliliters of water fill a cup? yes (no)
3. Circle the greater amount: (10 kilograms) 100 grams
4. Could someone's hand be 1 decimeter long? (yes) no
5. Circle the larger amount: 2 kilometers   (200 meters)
6. 1 meter = __1,000__ centimeters.
7. 1 kilometer = __100__ meters.
8. __1,000__ milliliters = 1 liter.
9. 100 meters = __10__ decimeter(s).
10. 5 grams = __500__ milligrams.
11. 20 meters = __2,000__ centimeters.
12. __300__ centimeters = 3 meters.
13. 1 metric ton = __1,000__ kilograms.
14. 1 gram = __1,000__ milligrams.
15. 10 kilometers = __100__ meters.
16. 10,000 milligrams = __1,000__ grams.

I'm sure I'll pass the test.

Will Ted pass? _____

Name

COOL DOWN, CLEAN UP

Athletes drink lots of refreshing drinks to cool down. To clean up, they take lots of showers and throw uniforms in the washer often.

Use estimation skills to solve these problems about their cool-down and clean up! Circle the answer that is the closest estimate.

1. Each athlete on the track team drinks about $3\frac{1}{2}$ gallons of water at each meet. There are 20 team members. How much water is drunk at each meet?

   54 cups   70 cups   540 cups   1,080 cups

2. There are 8 tug-of-war teams with 20 players each. Every player uses 2 towels for a shower. It takes $\frac{1}{10}$ C soap powder to wash each towel. How many gallons of soap are needed to wash the towels?

   16 gal   42 gal   2 gal   32 gal

3. Each drinking cup in the locker room gets filled with $\frac{1}{4}$ cup of ice. At the last game, 6 quarts of ice were divided among the cups. How many drinking cups were used?

   100   24   140   240

4. After a game, the football team uses plenty of deodorant. Each player uses 2.4 g under each arm. There are 30 players. How much deodorant is used for 10 games?

   150 kg   600 kg   15 kg   1.5 kg

5. Each thirsty runner at a race drinks about 800 milliliters of SLAM Sports Drink. If 102 runners show up for the race, how many 10-liter jugs of the drink are needed?

   80   8   1   10

6. The Booster Club earned money by starting a uniform-washing service. The washing machines, water, and electricity were furnished as a donation. They only had to buy soap, which cost 12 cents per uniform. They charged $5 per uniform. Over the season, they washed 88 uniforms. About how much profit did they make?

   $60 $440 $429 $45

7. At the end of the season, 98 pairs of smelly socks were left in lockers. Coach Brant decided to burn them. He threw one sock at a time into the fire. Each took $\frac{3}{4}$ minute to burn. About how long did it take all the socks to burn?

   5 hr $1\frac{1}{4}$ hr $2\frac{1}{2}$ hrs   4 hrs

8. Dusty wore out 14 pairs of running shoes over her 4 years of running cross-country races in high school. She ran a total of 4,200,000 meters during that time. How much mileage, on average, did she get from each pair of shoes?

   600 km   3,000 km   1,500 km   300 km

Name

TEARS ALLOWED

Tears are unavoidable at an onion-eating competition. Yes, people actually race to eat raw onions—all in hopes of setting new records.

Review the table with information about the number of onions eaten at a 2-minute competition. Represent this data on the line plot. X = 1 competitor.

Onions Eaten at Competition

Name	# of Onions	Name	# of Onions	Name	# of Onions
Amee	$\frac{1}{2}$	Lou	$2\frac{1}{2}$	Denise	1
Lasa	$4\frac{1}{2}$	Maya	$2\frac{1}{2}$	Harry	$2\frac{1}{2}$
Georgio	6	Tasha	2	Ramon	$2\frac{1}{2}$
Lane	2	DeShaun	2	Sue	$4\frac{1}{4}$
Tomas	$1\frac{1}{2}$	Evan	1	Jenna	$5\frac{1}{2}$
Marita	$5\frac{1}{2}$	Scott	$5\frac{1}{2}$	Kris	3
Anya	$5\frac{1}{2}$	Ryan	$3\frac{1}{2}$	Lucy	$5\frac{1}{2}$
Blake	$4\frac{1}{2}$	Lee	3	Todd	$5\frac{1}{2}$
Chou	$\frac{1}{2}$	Vonna	$4\frac{1}{2}$	Rob	5

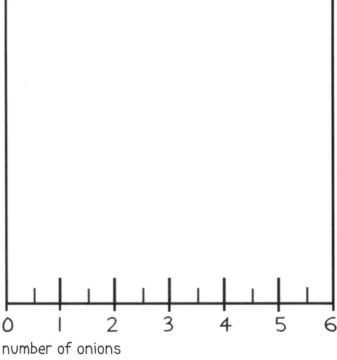

Onion-Eating Competition

number of onions

Name _____

THE LIFE SPAN OF BUBBLES

Believe it or not—someone has built a wall entirely out of bubbles! Fan-Yang of Canada built a 156-foot long, record-setting bubble wall in 1997. Unfortunately, bubbles have a short life span, so the wall did not last long!

The line plot shows how long some individual bubbles lasted in a bubble-blowing competition. Use data from it to answer the questions.

1. How many bubbles lasted $\frac{4}{5}$ minute? _____

2. How many bubbles lasted fewer than $\frac{2}{5}$ minute? _____

3. How many bubbles lasted 36 seconds? _____

4. How many bubbles lasted longer than 30 seconds? _____

5. How many bubbles are represented on the graph? _____

6. What time lengths show the same number of bubbles? _____
   _____

7. What pattern can be seen in the data?
   _____
   _____

Lasting Length of Bubbles

	$\frac{1}{10}$	$\frac{2}{10}$	$\frac{3}{10}$	$\frac{4}{10}$	$\frac{5}{10}$	$\frac{6}{10}$	$\frac{7}{10}$	$\frac{8}{10}$	$\frac{9}{10}$	1
					X					
				X	X					
				X	X	X				
			X	X	X	X				
			X	X	X	X	X			
X	X	X	X	X	X	X	X			
X	X	X	X	X	X	X	X	X		
X	X	X	X	X	X	X	X	X	X	

time in minutes

Name _____

DEEP-SEA DATA

These scuba divers have discovered treasure and are carrying it in small amounts up to the boat. The line plot shows data about the weight carried to the boat each trip.

Each X on the line plot represents one trip by a diver.
Use the data shown to answer the questions.

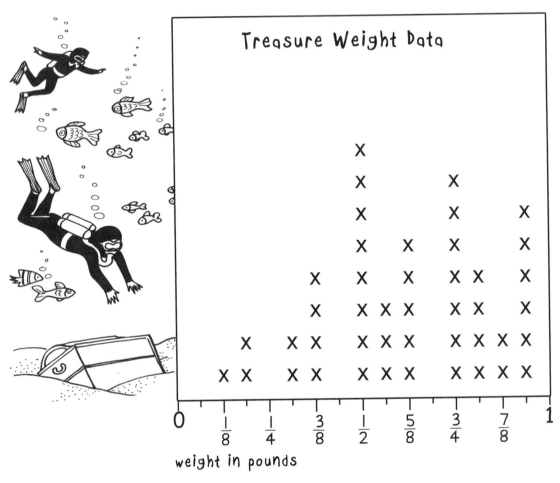

1. How many trips to the boat are shown in this data? _____

2. What is the difference between the greatest weight and least weight carried? _____

3. In how many trips did a diver carry more than $\frac{12}{16}$ pound? _____

4. How many times was $\frac{9}{16}$ pound of treasure carried? _____

5. In how many trips did a diver carry 5 ounces? _____

6. In how many trips did a diver carry $\frac{13}{16}$ pound? _____

Use with page 97.

Name _____

On the next boat trip to the treasure site, divers carried more loads of gold coins and jewels to the boat.

Ali	$\frac{4}{5}$
Karin	$\frac{5}{10}$
Lisel	$1\frac{9}{10}$
Devon	$1\frac{2}{5}$
Dana	$1\frac{5}{10}$
Kaylee	$1\frac{1}{10}$
Sarah	$1\frac{2}{5}$
Mikel	$\frac{5}{10}$
Sun Lei	$1\frac{2}{5}$
D.J.	$\frac{3}{10}$
Will	$\frac{4}{5}$
Zoe	$1\frac{2}{5}$
Misha	$\frac{4}{5}$
Anna	$1\frac{5}{10}$
Lily	$1\frac{1}{10}$
Gabe	$1\frac{2}{5}$
Zach	$\frac{1}{10}$
Aalyah	$1\frac{1}{10}$
Kobe	$\frac{4}{5}$
Diego	$1\frac{7}{10}$
Ramon	$1\frac{1}{10}$
Lucia	$1\frac{5}{10}$
Caitlin	$1\frac{2}{5}$
Keisha	$\frac{4}{5}$
Ava	$\frac{1}{5}$
Gianna	$1\frac{7}{10}$

The list shows divers' names and the weights they carried.
Record this data on the line plot.
Use an X to represent each diver.

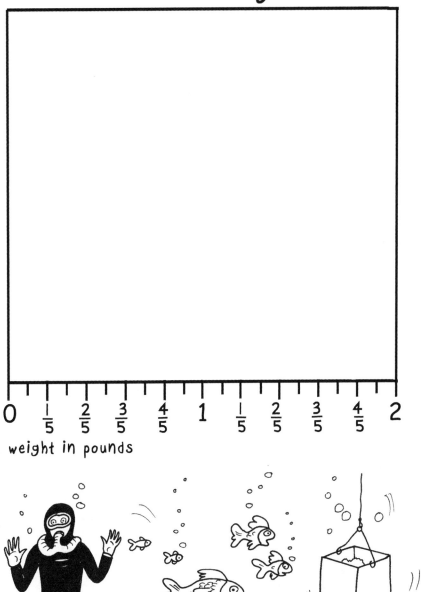

The Treasure They Carried

0    $\frac{1}{5}$ $\frac{2}{5}$ $\frac{3}{5}$ $\frac{4}{5}$ 1 $\frac{1}{5}$ $\frac{2}{5}$ $\frac{3}{5}$ $\frac{4}{5}$ 2

weight in pounds

Use with page 96.

Name

CRAZY COMPETITIONS

People do lots of weird tricks in competition! The clock is ticking while they kill mosquitoes, juggle flaming torches, spit watermelon seeds, toss and spin pizza dough, and other wacky feats! A family of pizza-dough tossers has many competitors. Cousins, mothers, grandparents, kids, aunts and uncles, and siblings all know the skill.

The line plot shows data for the height to which these relatives can throw the dough. Use the data to answer the questions.

1. How many relatives throw the dough higher than 34 ft, 3 inches? _____

2. What is the difference between the greatest and least height shown? _____

3. Which heights have the same number of tosses? _____

   _____

4. How many relatives throw between 31 and 32 inches? _____

5. J.J. throws $30\frac{1}{2}$ inches. How many others throw the same or within $\frac{1}{2}$ inch of her? _____

6. How many relatives are included in the data? _____

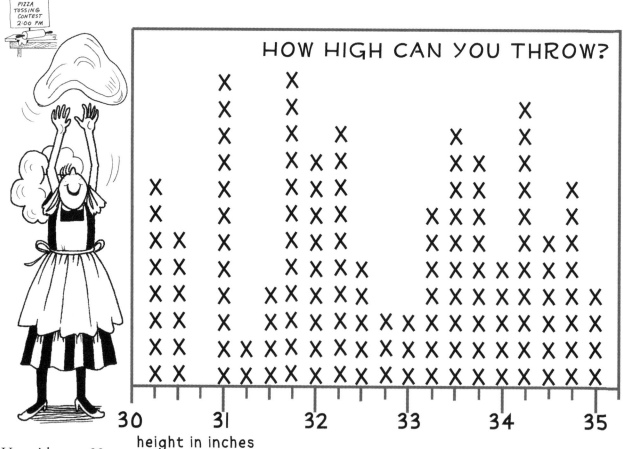

Use with page 99.

Name

In 2008, a competitor named Humble Bob set a record at the Skyline Chili Spaghetti Eat-Off in Ohio. He ate $11\frac{1}{2}$ pounds of spaghetti in 10 minutes.

The line plot shows some data about weight of spaghetti eaten in another contest. Each X stands for one competitor.

1. How many ate between $2\frac{1}{2}$ and $2\frac{7}{10}$ kg? _____

2. How many ate more than $2\frac{4}{5}$ kg? _____

3. Which amounts of spaghetti had the same number of eaters? _____

   _____

4. How many ate $2\frac{7}{20}$ kg? _____

5. What amount had four different eaters? _____

6. How many eaters are represented in the data? _____

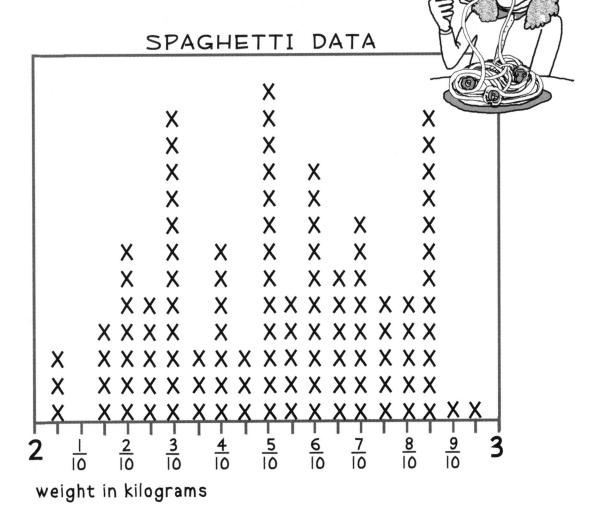

SPAGHETTI DATA

weight in kilograms

Use with page 98.

Name _____

GET A JUMP ON VOLUME

The skateboard club has some very talented competitors. They practice year-round on ramps and jumps in the new skateboard park. Here are some of the structures they have built to jump over.

**Examine each structure to find its volume.
(Count the cubic units.) Then answer the questions.**

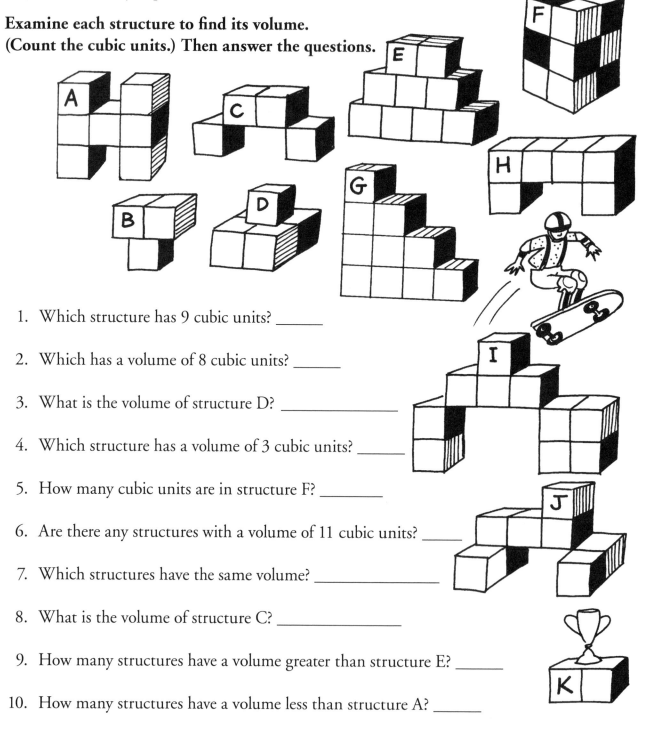

1. Which structure has 9 cubic units? _____

2. Which has a volume of 8 cubic units? _____

3. What is the volume of structure D? _____

4. Which structure has a volume of 3 cubic units? _____

5. How many cubic units are in structure F? _____

6. Are there any structures with a volume of 11 cubic units? _____

7. Which structures have the same volume? _____

8. What is the volume of structure C? _____

9. How many structures have a volume greater than structure E? _____

10. How many structures have a volume less than structure A? _____

Use with page 101.

Name

Continue your examination of skateboard structures that you began on page 100. Find the volume of one more structure. Then create some of your own.

11. What is the volume of structure L? _____

12. Add to structure L to increase its volume to 31 cubic units.

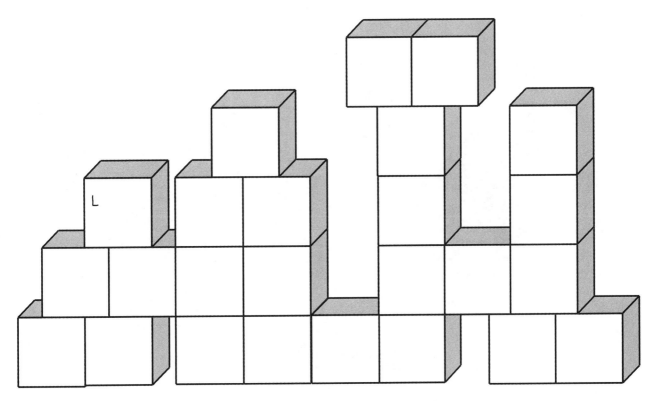

L

Use with page 100.

Name _____

GEOMETRY ON WHEELS

The practice course for the skating team is loaded with geometric space figures. Skaters practice jumps and turns over and around the figures.

Solve the problems about obstacles on the course.

1. Find the volume of an obstacle with measurements of 3 feet by 1 foot by $\frac{1}{2}$ foot.

2. Find the volume of a figure that has six faces with all its edges 7 inches long.

3. One obstacle has a length of 20 inches, a width of 10 inches, and a volume of 3,000 cubic inches. What is its height?

4. Find the volume of an obstacle with measurements of 0.5 meters by 1.2 meters by 1 meter.

5. An obstacle has a volume of 48,000 cubic centimeters. Its height is 12 centimeters, and its width is 50 centimeters. What is its length?

6. The final obstacle has a width of 10 inches, a length of 20 inches, and a volume of 3,000 cubic inches. Could its height be 16 inches?

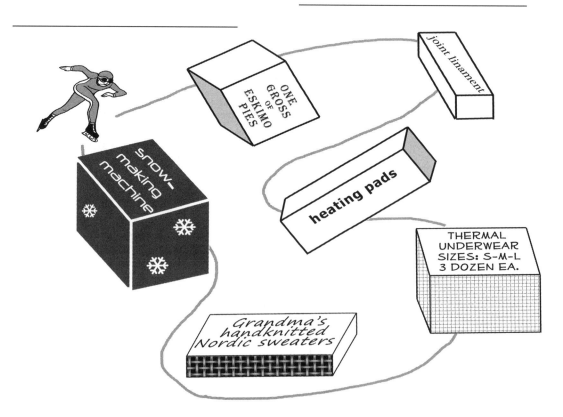

Name

HUNGRY FANS

The game has gone into overtime, and the fans are extremely hungry! They are going to need a lot of snacks before the night is over.

Find the volume of each container to discover who got the most to eat or drink. Answer questions A and B at the bottom of the page. Assume all containers are packed full of whatever ingredient is inside.

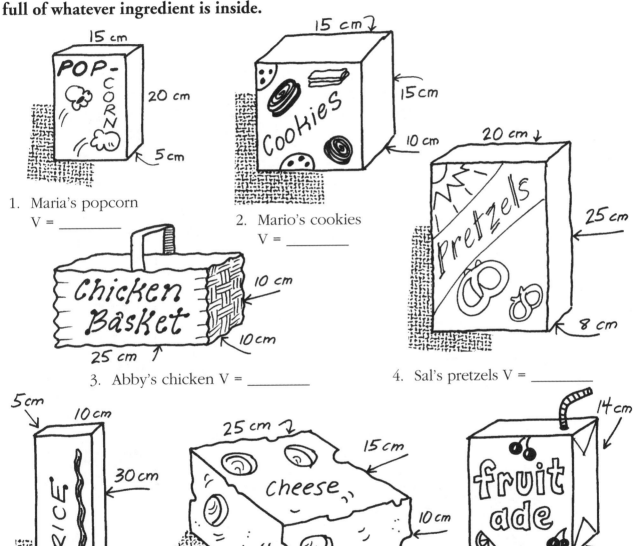

1. Maria's popcorn
   V = _____

2. Mario's cookies
   V = _____

3. Abby's chicken V = _____

4. Sal's pretzels V = _____

5. Val's licorice
   V = _____

6. Evan's cheese
   V = _____

7. Angie's drink
   V = _____

A. Which two fans ate the same volume of snacks?_____

B. Which fan ate or drank the greatest volume?_____

Name_____

UNIFORM MEASUREMENTS

Al, the athletic director, is confused. He is passing out boxes of uniforms but doesn't know which one to give to each coach.

Identify each coach's box from the description the coach gives. Fill in the blanks on this page and the next page (page 105) with the letter of the correct box.

1. *My box is 1 x 1 x 2 feet. My cheerleading uniforms are in box _____ .*

2. *The measurements of my box are 5 x 36 x 5 inches. My swimmer's uniforms are in box _____ .*

3. *My football uniforms are in the box that is 15 x 33 x 11 inches. This is box _____ .*

4. *My box measures 30 x 4 x 15 inches. The track uniforms are in box _____ .*

A. $V = 1620$ in³

B. $V = 3024$ in³

C. $V = 1800$ in³

D. $V = 2$ ft³

Use with page 105.

Name

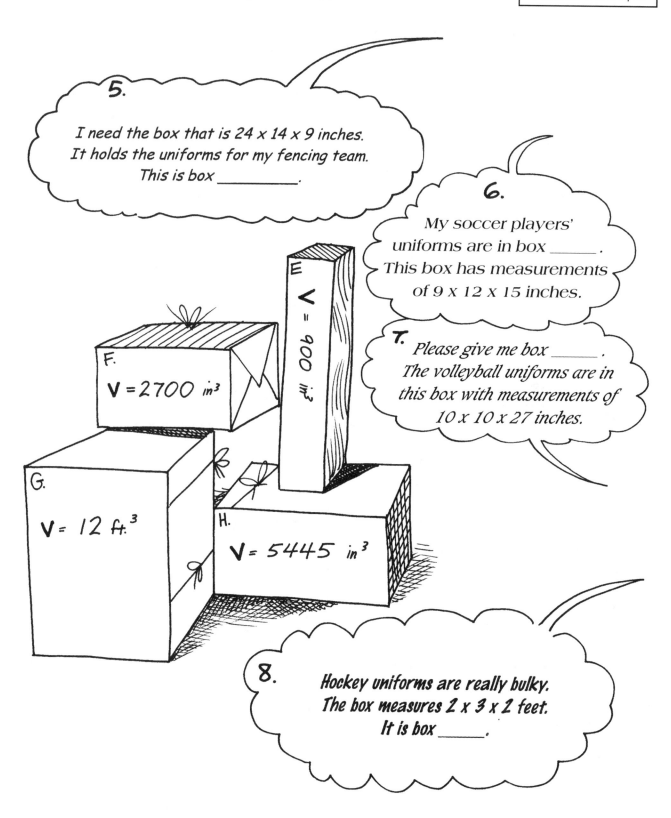

5. I need the box that is 24 x 14 x 9 inches. It holds the uniforms for my fencing team. This is box _____.

6. My soccer players' uniforms are in box _____. This box has measurements of 9 x 12 x 15 inches.

7. Please give me box _____. The volleyball uniforms are in this box with measurements of 10 x 10 x 27 inches.

8. Hockey uniforms are really bulky. The box measures 2 x 3 x 2 feet. It is box _____.

F. V = 2700 in³

E. V = 900 in³

G. V = 12 ft.³

H. V = 5445 in³

Which uniforms need the biggest box? _____

Use with page 104.

Name _____

THINK INSIDE THE BOX

Volume is space inside a three-dimensional figure—measured in cubic units. Axel wonders what will fit in this box. He can figure that out by stacking it full of cubes. Or, he can measure it and use a volume formula—or both!

Find two boxes and a large set of measuring cubes or cube-shaped building blocks. (Find cubes. Measure them so you know the unit. Or use the pattern below to make lots of cubes.) Fill each box with cubes. Then count them! Write the volume by giving the number of cubes.

After you have done this, use a measuring tool to measure all three dimensions of each box. Use the volume formula for a rectangle to calculate the volume of the box. Compare the two measurements.

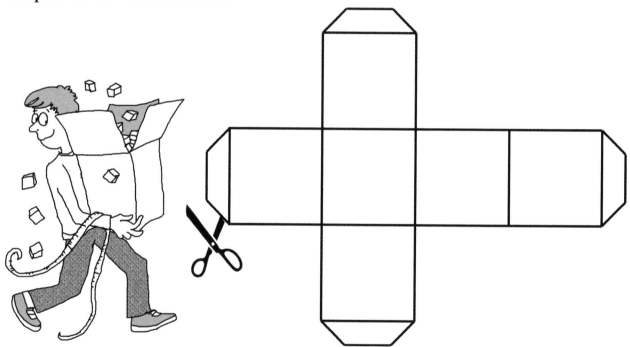

Box #1	Box #2
1. Cubic unit used to measure:	1. Cubic unit used to measure:
_____	_____
How many? _____	How many? _____
2. Measurements with tool:	2. Measurements with tool:
_____ by _____ by _____ (unit)	_____ by _____ by _____ (unit)
V = _____	V = _____

Name

GEOMETRY

Grade 5

THE THINGS PEOPLE THROW

It's amazing what things get thrown, tossed, and spit in an effort to set a record! Some of the world records include spitting cherry pits and crickets, tossing pancakes and cow pies, and catching tossed grapes in the mouth.

The table shows information about other things tossed in contests. Find the tossed items on the graph below. Write the locations where items are found. Write (x, y).

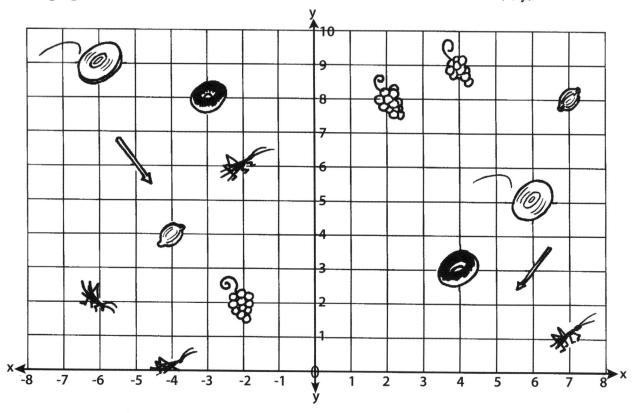

1. The 🍇 are found at _____ , _____ , and _____ .

2. The 🥔 are found at _____ and _____ .

3. The 🥯 are found at _____ and _____ .

4. The 🥞 are found at _____ and _____ .

5. The ↘ are found at _____ and _____ .

6. The 🦗 are found at _____ , _____ , _____ , and _____ .

Use with page 109.

Name

Page 108 showed some things people throw in competitions. But there's more! Have fun locating some other things that get tossed!

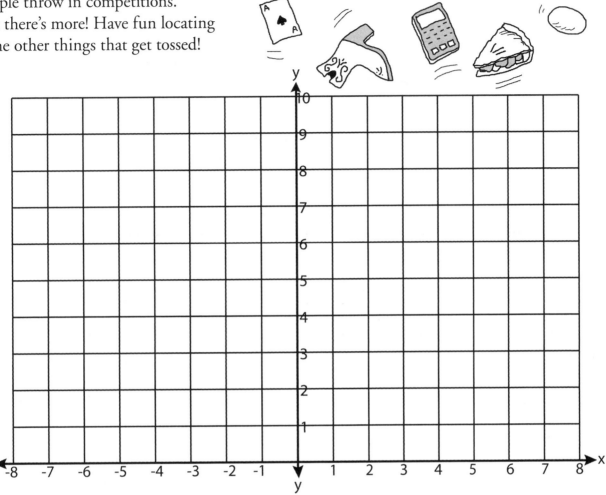

Draw the following items at the locations (coordinates) shown.

1. Draw eggs at (0, -3) and (7, 4).

2. Draw a pie at (-5, 5).

3. Draw hats at (3, 4) and (-6, 9).

4. Draw paint splats at (1, 0) and (0, 10).

5. Draw a cell phone at (-2, 2).

6. Draw a dead fish at (-6, 2).

7. Draw chopsticks at (8, 0).

8. Draw a pie at (-5, 5).

9. Draw an iPod at (2, 8).

10. Draw boots at (-3, 0) and (8, 5).

11. Draw an ant at (-2, 2).

12. Draw a sword extending from (5, 0) to (5, 6).

Use with page 108.

Name

DOZENS OF DANCERS

Dancers around the world try to set records for the longest or fastest dance, or for the dance with the most people. The biggest tap dance, with 6,654 dancers, took place in New York City. The longest line dance had 5,502 dancers. The longest dancing dragon was made up of 2,431 people.

These dancers are making their line around a coordinate grid. Write the coordinates of each dancer on the grid. Write coordinates like this: (x, y).

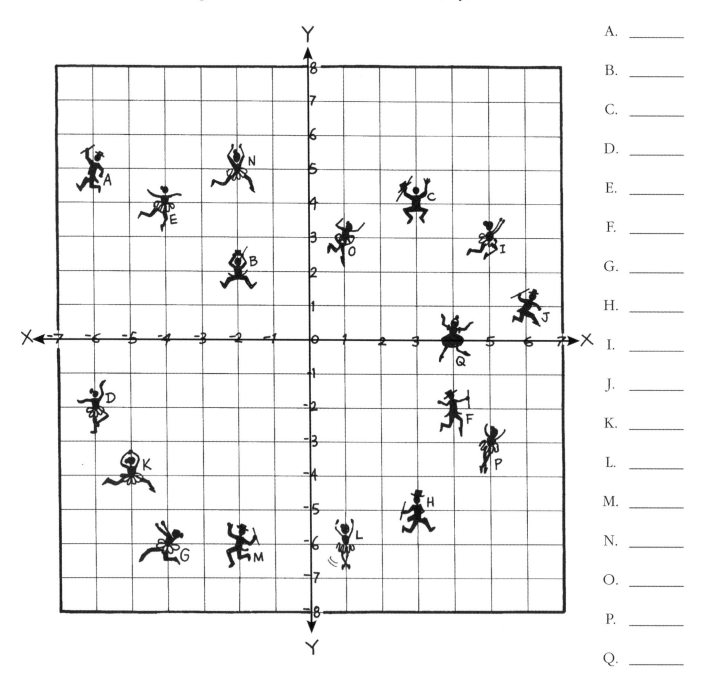

A. _____

B. _____

C. _____

D. _____

E. _____

F. _____

G. _____

H. _____

I. _____

J. _____

K. _____

L. _____

M. _____

N. _____

O. _____

P. _____

Q. _____

Name

A RECORD-HOLDING CRAWLER

This character holds a record with a best time of 2 minutes, 30 seconds on a circular track. He's in the record books for a racing championship held every year in England. What is the record?

Follow the directions to plot and connect the points on the grid. You'll find out who or what the racer is.

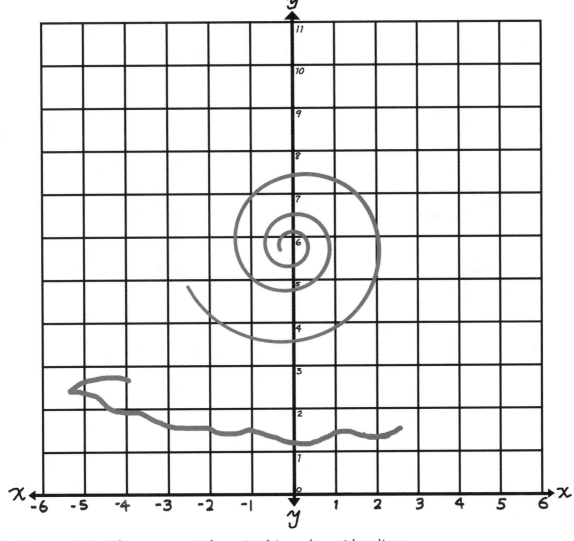

Plot these points. Then connect them in this order with a line.

A. (3, 1)	F. (5, 9)	K. (2, 2)	P. (−3, 7)
B. (4, 2)	G. (4, 11)	L. (−2, 2)	Q. (−2, 9)
C. (4, 3)	H. (4, 9)	M. (−3, 3)	R. (0, 10)
D. (5, 8)	I. (3, 7)	N. (−4, 4)	S. (2, 9)
E. (6, 10)	J. (3, 4)	O. (−3, 5)	T. (3, 7)

Name _____

THE HIGHEST RECORDS

Some of the most spectacular mountain-climbing records were set on Mt. Everest, the world's highest mountain. On one May day in 1993, forty climbers from ten different countries reached the summit of Everest. This is still the record for the most to summit Everest in one day. Apa Sherpa holds the record for climbing Everest the most times. As of May 2011, he had reached the summit 21 times. He does these climbs without using bottled oxygen.

Follow the trail of two climbers. Plot the points for each climber on the graph on page 113. Then draw a line to show each climber's path for the ascent up the mountain.

1. Color these points RED for Helena's path. If a point is not already there, add it in RED. Then join them with a RED line in the order listed below.

A	(−2, −12)	I	(−3, −5)	R	(1, 2)
B	(−6, −11)	J	(−1, −4)	S	(3, 3)
C	(−1, −10)	K	(−6, −3)	T	(4, 5)
D	(−3, −9)	L	(−7, −1)	U	(2, 6)
E	(−1, −8)	M	(−5 −1)	V	(−2, 6)
F	(−5, −8)	N	(−6, 0)	W	(−1, 8)
G	(−3, −7)	O	(−5, 1)	X	(−1, 10)
H	(−5, −6)	P	(−3, 1)	Y	(0, 12)
		Q	(−1, 2)		

2. Color these points BLUE for Peter's path. Then join them with a BLUE line in the order listed below.

A	(4, −12)	M	(−1, −1)
B	(4, −10)	N	(−3, 1)
C	(2, −10)	O	(3, 1)
D	(4, −8)	P	(6, 4)
E	(5, −9)	Q	(−4, 3)
F	(6, −8)	R	(−5, 4)
G	(9, −6)	S	(−4, 6)
H	(6, −6)	T	(−1, 7)
I	(5, −4)	U	(2, 8)
J	(7, −2)	V	(2, 10)
K	(3, −3)	W	(1, 11)
L	(−3, −2)	X	(0, 12)

Use with page 113.

Name

Follow the directions on page 112 to draw the paths for the two mountain climbers.

3. How many times did the climbers' paths touch or cross? _____

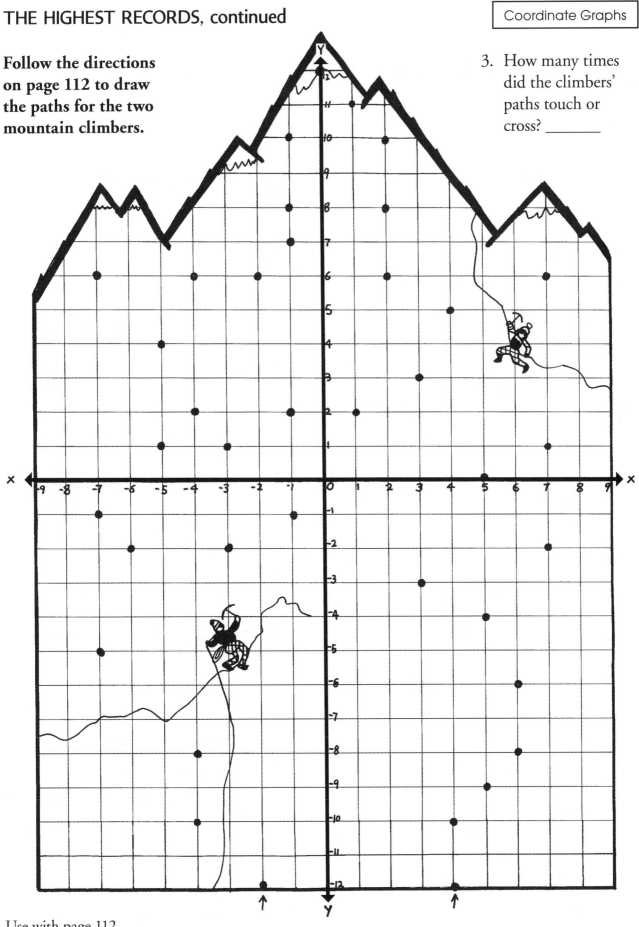

Use with page 112.

Name

EIGHT HOURS OF SHOE SHINING

Imagine shining almost 15,000 shoes! A team of four teenagers set the record for shoe shining by polishing 14,975 shoes in London, England.

Decide what some of those shoes looked like. Draw them on the grid in the locations that are described below.

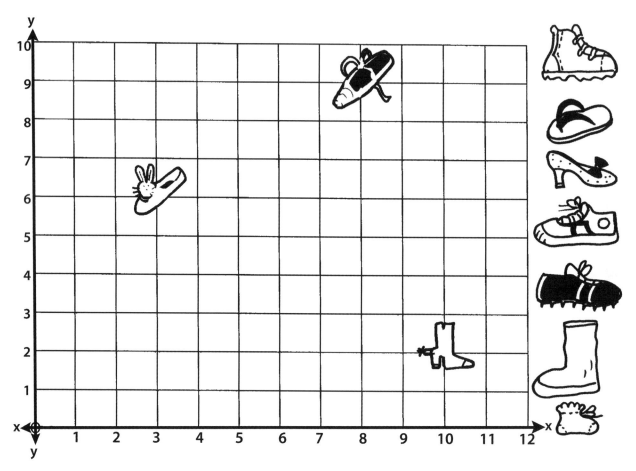

1. Is the bunny slipper at (3, 6)? _____
2. Where is the ballet shoe? _____
3. Where is the cowboy boot? _____
4. Draw a clown shoe at (0, 3).
5. Draw a tennis shoe at (2, 9).
6. Draw a baby shoe at (4, 3).
7. Draw a blue dancing shoe at (6, 7).
8. Draw a brown hiking boot at (1, 9).
9. Draw a green slipper at (5, 7).
10. Draw a red high heel at (9, 5).
11. Draw one of your shoes at (8, 4).
12. Draw a loafer at (8, 0).
13. Draw any yellow shoe at (11, 1).
14. Draw any purple shoe at (5, 0).
15. Draw any orange shoe at (7, 5).
16. Draw a fancy shoe at (11, 6).
17. Draw any shoe at (2, 2).
18. Draw any shoe at (1, 6).

Name

CURIOUS COLLECTIONS

It's amazing what people collect! There are some stunning record-setting collections. But many people just collect for the fun of it!

Here are some things people collect. Draw them in at the locations (coordinates) described.

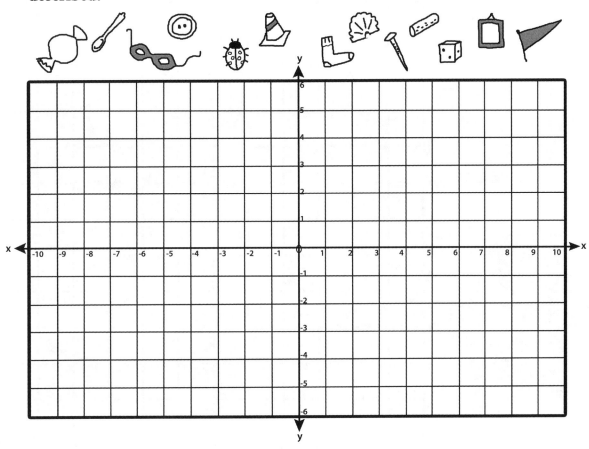

1. Draw a picture frame at (4, 0).

2. Draw buttons at (6, 2) and (-5, 3).

3. Draw a ladybug earring at (-5, -5).

4. Draw a pennant at (10, 4).

5. Draw a taffy candy at (3, 6).

6. Draw a sock at (-8, 5).

7. Draw a die (one of a pair of dice) at (-1, -1).

8. Draw gumballs at (-8, -5), (0, -6), and (8, -4).

9. Draw seashells at (-3, 5), (5, 4), and (2, -4).

10. Draw chalk at (-3, -4).

11. Draw nails at (0, 4) and (-4, 0).

12. Draw a safety pin at (2, -4).

13. Draw toothpaste from (1, -1) to (6, 2).

14. Draw a parking meter from (-7, -2) to (-7, 3).

Name

SWATTING TO SET A RECORD

Yes, there really is a World Mosquito-Killing Championship. It is held every year in Finland. Henri Pellonpää holds the record for the greatest number of these pesky insects killed in five minutes. His record is 21 mosquitoes.

Follow the directions below to locate Henri's mosquitoes on the coordinate grid.

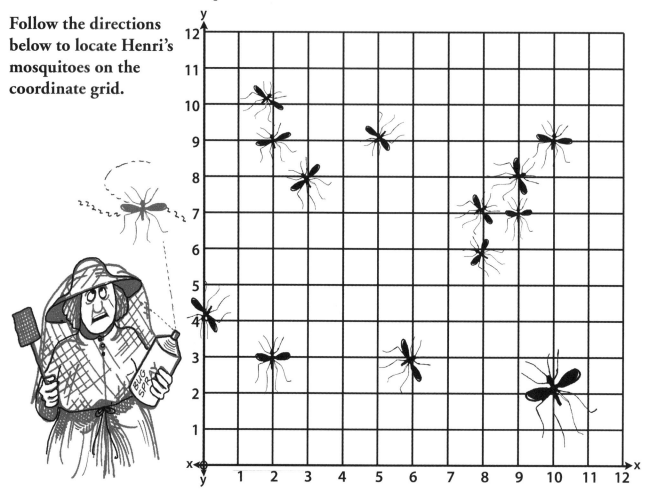

Remember that coordinates of a location are written (x, y).
X is the location on the horizontal line. Y is the location on the vertical line.

1. Is there a mosquito at (8, 6)? _____

2. Is there a mosquito at (2, 10)? _____

3. Is there a mosquito at (9, 4)? _____

4. Is there a mosquito at (10, 8)? _____

5. Is there a mosquito at (12, 0)? _____

6. Is there a mosquito at (9, 7)? _____

7. Is there a mosquito at (8, 7)? _____

8. Is there a mosquito at (3, 6)? _____

9. Is there a mosquito at (6, 3)? _____

10. Where is the largest mosquito? _____

11. Draw a mosquito at (12, 3).

12. Draw a mosquito at (3, 6).

13. Draw a mosquito at (9, 4).

14. Draw a mosquito at (8, 0).

Use with page 117.

Name

Others try to set records setting different creeping, crawling, flying critters. Follow directions to add these critters to the graph.

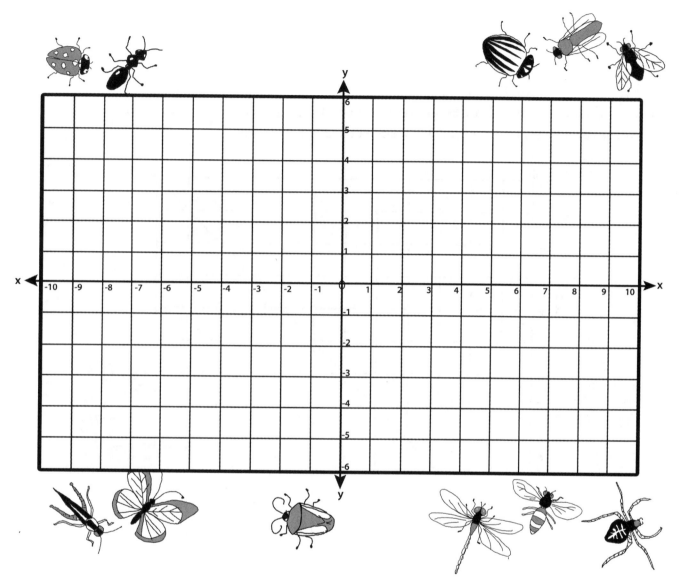

1. Draw spiders at (2, 6), (7, -2), (-7, 0), and (-4, -6)

2. Draw flies at (-2, -3) and (9, 3).

3. Draw dragonflies at (5, -4) and (-10, 4).

4. Draw beetles at (0, -5), (-5, 5) and (1, 0).

5. Draw bees at (-2, 3) and (-10, -6).

6. Draw ants at (8, 0) and (-8, -4).

7. Draw crickets at (-6, 4) and (2, -3).

Draw your own creatures at points on the graph. Name the creature. Write the coordinates.

Creature	Coordinates
8. _____	(___,___)
9. _____	(___,___)
10. _____	(___,___)
11. _____	(___,___)

Use with page 116.

Name _____

Common Core Reinforcement Activities — 5th Grade Math

NONSTOP BOUNCING

Some people spend hours on a pogo stick. Many of them even compete to see who can jump the most or travel the farthest! In 2011, James Roumeliotis of the USA jumped 206,864 times in 20 hours and 13 seconds.

The graph shows the bouncing patterns of one pogo stick traveler. This athlete increased the number of miles she traveled on her pogo stick with each month of training for a year. Use the graph to answer the questions.

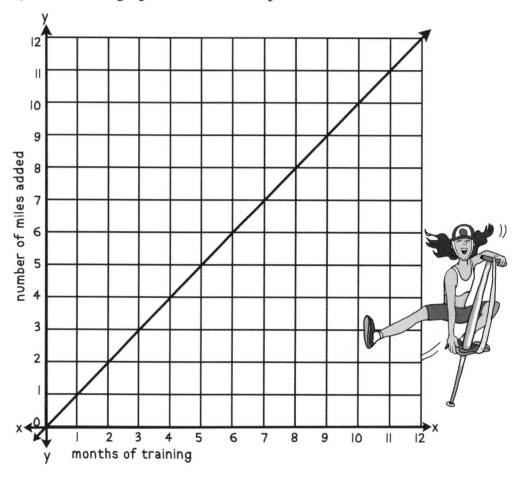

1. How many miles did Chaundra add by the end of month 3? (Remember that the graph shows how many she added each month to the previous month.)

2. How many miles did Chaundra add by the end of month 6?

3. How many miles did Chaundra add by the end of month 4?

4. At the start of the year, Chaundra could travel 3 miles with continuous bouncing and only brief rests. How many miles did she travel in her final month of this year of training?

5. If this pattern continued for a total of 15 months, how many miles would you expect her to travel in month 15?

Name

SERIOUS ABOUT TATTOOS

Imagine a body completely covered with tattoos. Julia Gnuse is the most tattooed woman in the world. She began getting colorful tattoos to cover a troublesome skin condition. Now, just about every inch of her body is covered.

Another fan of tattoos, Laticia, kept a graph of the tattoos she got each from the year of her first tattoo through her twelfth year of this practice. Use information from the graph to answer the questions about her tattoos.

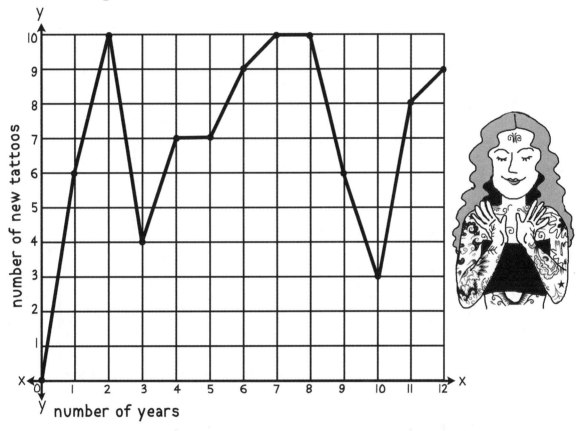

1. On the graph, what is the meaning of the coordinates (8, 10)? _____ _____

2. What was the change in number of tattoos from year 10 to year 12? _____

3. How many tattoos did she have by the end of year 9? _____

4. On the graph, what is the meaning of the coordinates (4, 7)? _____ _____

5. On the graph, what year has the coordinates (0, 9)? _____

6. What two sets of coordinates show the greatest drop in number of tattoos from one year to the next?_____

7. Give two sets of coordinates that show no change in the number from one year to the next. _____

8. How many tattoos did she have by the end of year 12? _____

Name _____

THE MISSING CORNERS

The graph was intended to plot four geometric figures. But they can't be finished, because each one has a missing corner. The search is on!

Use your sharp graphing skills to find the missing corners for some shapes on the grid.

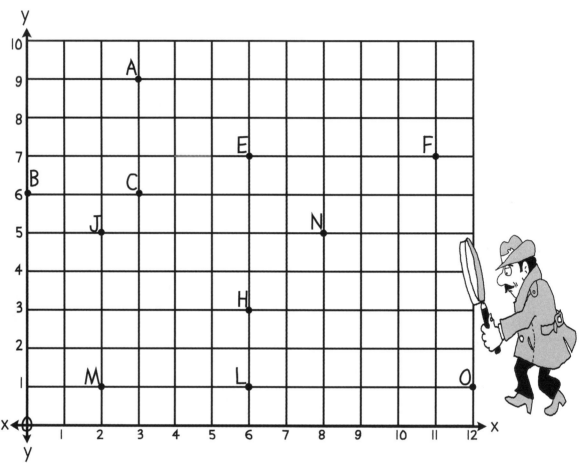

1. Parallelogram ABCD is missing corner D. Where is it? _____

   Plot the point, label it, and write the coordinates. Then finish drawing the figure.

2. Rectangle EFGH is missing corner G. Where is it? _____

   Plot the point, label it, and write the coordinates. Then finish drawing the figure.

3. Square JKLM is missing corner K. Where is it? _____

   Plot the point, label it, and write the coordinates. Then finish drawing the figure.

4. Right triangle NOP is missing corner P. Where is it? _____

   Plot the point, label it, and write the coordinates. Then finish drawing the figure.

Name _____

120

SIGNS FROM THE CROWD

These football fans are showing off some of their knowledge about geometry. Figure out if they know their geometry well while you show what you know.

Choose a word or phrase from the center list that matches each sign. Write the letter(s) in the blank on the sign.

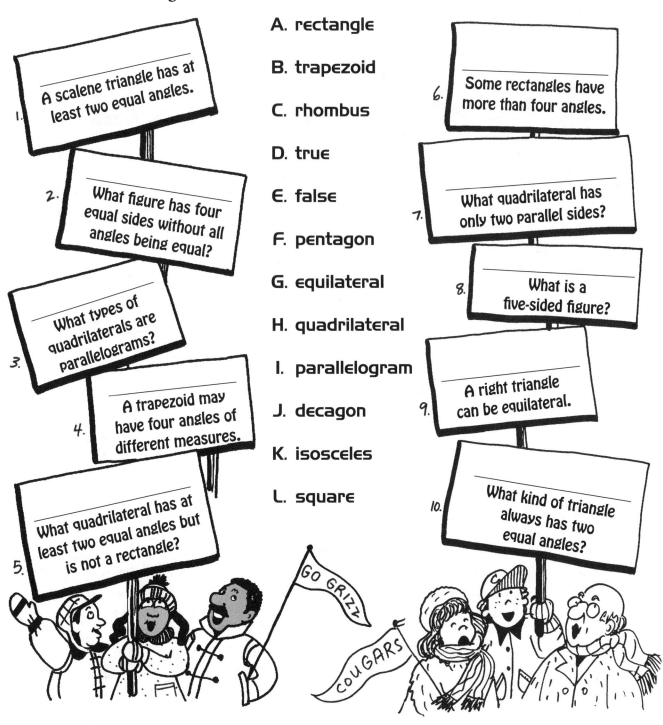

A. rectangle

B. trapezoid

C. rhombus

D. true

E. false

F. pentagon

G. equilateral

H. quadrilateral

I. parallelogram

J. decagon

K. isosceles

L. square

1. A scalene triangle has at least two equal angles.

2. What figure has four equal sides without all angles being equal?

3. What types of quadrilaterals are parallelograms?

4. A trapezoid may have four angles of different measures.

5. What quadrilateral has at least two equal angles but is not a rectangle?

6. Some rectangles have more than four angles.

7. What quadrilateral has only two parallel sides?

8. What is a five-sided figure?

9. A right triangle can be equilateral.

10. What kind of triangle always has two equal angles?

GO GRIZZ

COUGARS

Name

A PLANE MESS

Coach Jackson teaches math when he is not coaching volleyball. He had some great posters ready for his geometry lesson today, but, as usual, he forgot to close the window. A huge wind blew his stuff all over the floor.

Get the definition posters back together with the math terms in time for class. Write the letter from the poster right below the matching term.

BANNER GEOMETRY

Geometry shows up in all kinds of places. Even the new team banner offers a good place for geometry review.

Look carefully at the figures within the banner. Follow the directions and answer the questions. Use letters at vertices to name figures.

1. Name an equilateral triangle on the banner. _____
   Explain what an equilateral triangle is. _____
   _____

2. Name an isosceles triangle on the banner. _____
   Explain what an isosceles triangle is. _____
   _____

3. Name a scalene triangle on the banner. _____
   Explain what an equilateral triangle is. _____
   _____

4. Name a right triangle. _____
   Explain what a right triangle is. _____
   _____

5. What kind of figure is SQRT? _____
   How do you know? _____

6. What kind of figure is SQRU? _____
   How do you know? _____

7. What kind of figure is the entire banner? _____

Name _____

THE FAMILY TREE

All the two-dimensional figures named below are related. They share a family tree; but they may fall on different branches.

Write the name of each figure where it belongs on the tree.

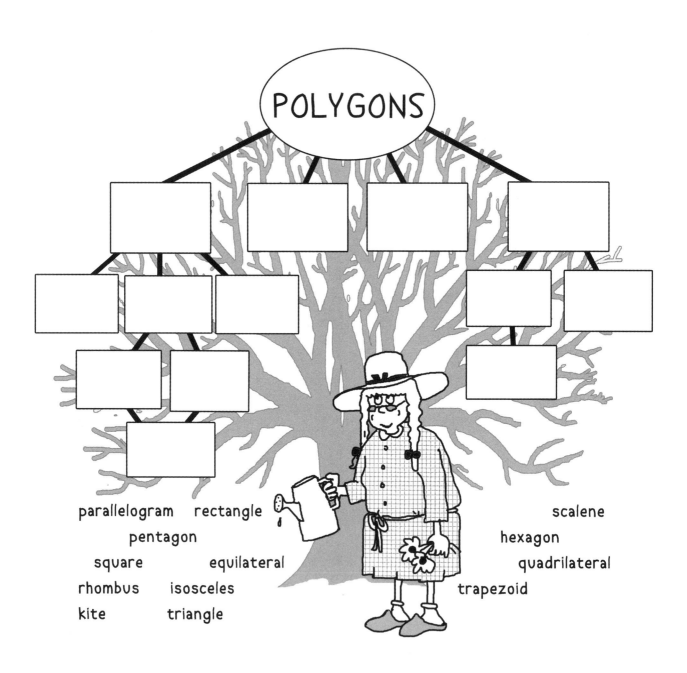

parallelogram   rectangle

pentagon

square   equilateral

rhombus   isosceles

kite   triangle

scalene

hexagon

quadrilateral

trapezoid

Name

GO FIGURE

It's easy to get figures confused, so you have to be sharp about their sides and angles. Figure out what's wrong with these confusing statements about two-dimensional figures!

**The table gives statements about different figures. Each statement has a problem.
Figure out and explain what's wrong with the statement.**

		What's Wrong?
1	A trapezoid has 2 parallel sides, so it must be a parallelogram.	
2	A trapezoid cannot have a right angle.	
3	A right triangle can be an equilateral triangle.	
4	A rhombus always has four right angles.	
5	A triangle can have two 60° angles and one 80° angle.	
6	A rectangle has four right angles, so it must be a square.	
7	A regular pentagon has congruent sides but non-congruent angles.	
8	A scalene triangle can have one right angle.	
9	The sum of the angles in a quadrilateral is 240°.	

Name _____

SHOW AND TELL

So you think you know all about plane figures (two-dimensional shapes)?
Show what you know. Turn a description into a drawing with a name!

Read each description. Draw the figure and tell what it is.

A. This figure has three
sides. Two are the
same length, but the
third is not.
Two angles are equal.
Show it. Tell its name.

_____

B. This figure has four
right angles. Two
of the sides are the
same length.
Show it. Tell its name.

_____

C. This figure has three
sides. None of the
angles are equal.
Show it. Tell its name.

_____

D. This quadrilateral
has two parallel sides,
but they are not
the same length.
There is one right angle.
Show it. Tell its name.

_____

E. This figure has four
sides and two pairs
of parallel sides. There
are no right angles.
Show it. Tell its name.

_____

F. This figure has four
sides of equal length,
but no right angles.
Show it. Tell its name.

_____

Name

ASSESSMENT & ANSWER KEYS

MATH ASSESSMENT

PART ONE: OPERATIONS AND ALGEBRAIC THINKING

Evaluate the expressions.

1. 10 x (35 + 8) = _____

2. (40 – 16) x 20 = _____

3. 15 + (120 ÷ 20) = _____

4. [(3 x 100) – 25] x 2 = _____

Find an expression on the sign that matches the words. Write the letter.

_____ 5. five times the sum of nine and six

_____ 6. half the difference between nine and six

_____ 7. Subtract ten from the product of six and nine. Multiply this by five.

_____ 8. Add five and six. Multiply this by nine.

_____ 9. Subtract the product of six and five from ninety.

Snowboarding Injuries

A. (5 + 6) x 9
B. 90 – (6 + 5)
C. (6 + 9) ÷ 5
D. 5 x (9 + 6)
E. 90 – (6 x 5)
F. (6 x 9) ÷ 5
G. (9 – 6) ÷ 2
H. [(6 x 9) –10] x 5

Use information from the table to complete 10–13.

Speed of Skiers	10 mph	20 mph	30 mph	40 mph	50 mph
Number of Injuries	2	4	8	16	32

10. Describe the pattern for the speed of skiers.

_____

_____

_____

11. Describe the pattern for the number of injuries.

_____

_____

_____

12. Describe the relationship between the two patterns.

_____

_____

_____

13. How many injuries would you expect to see for the group of skiers moving at 60 mph? _____

Evaluate the expressions.

14. two less than 85 = _____

15. eight more than the square of 3 = _____

16. ten less than the product of 4 and 15 = _____

17. twice the square of 9 = _____

18. twelve less than 80 divided by 5 = _____

Name

PART TWO: NUMBER AND OPERATIONS IN BASE TEN

Write an answer.

1. Which distance contains 69 tens?

_____

2. Which distance contains 20 hundreds?

_____

3. How many tens are represented by the 7 in the polar sled ride distance?

_____

4. How many thousands are represented by the 3 in the walk?

_____

5. How many hundreds are represented by the 4 in the wheelchair ride?

_____

Circle the correct answer.

6. Which represents the distance of the backward walk?

   8×10^4 8×10^3 8×10^2

7. When you multiply a number by ten to the fifth power, how many zeros should you add?

   two   three   four   five   six

8. What is the product: 45×10^4?

   90,000   450,000   45,000   0.0045

9. What is the quotient: $600,000 \div 10^3$?

   600,000,000   600   6,000   60,000

10. What is the numeral for six and sixty-three thousandths?

   0.0663   6.603   6.0063   6.063

STRANGE JOURNEYS
Approximate Distances of Record

Journey	Miles
taxi ride	21,691
polar sled ride	3,750
lawnmower ride	3,366
backwards walk	8,000
snowmobile ride	10,252
wheelchair ride	24,901
backwards run	3,100
walk	32,202
walk on stilts	2,008
unicycle ride	3,261
leapfrog trip	996

Write an explanation.

11. When 8.054 is multiplied by 10^3, what happens to the decimal point?

   _____

   _____

12. When 8,024.302 is divided by 10^4, what happens to the decimal point?

   _____

   _____

Write >, <, or = in the blank.

13.   9.026   _____   9.0926

14.   0.0550   _____   0.055

15.   11.0101   _____   11.1011

16.   66.92   _____   66.0999

Write the numeral.

17. $(5 \times 10,000) + (1 \times 100) + 6 =$

   _____

Name

Compare the distances.

18. Felix leapt 103.054 feet. Frankie leapt 103.504 feet. Who leapt farthest?

_____

19. Freddie leapt 4.6978 meters. Fifi leapt 4.6879 meters. Who leapt farthest?

_____

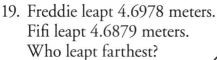

20. Felicity traveled 18.078 meters. Round this to the nearest hundredth.

_____

21. Francie traveled 13.0529 meters. Round this to the nearest thousandth.

_____

Solve the problems.

22. 1,488 frogs took part in the leapfrog contest. The competitors were divided into 62 groups. How many frogs were in each group?

_____

23. Arnie took part in 12 sword-swallowing competitions a month for 4 full years. How many competitions did he attend?

_____

24.   117
      x 35

25.   2,613
      x 206

26. 31)930

27. 18)5583

28. Each frog team leaps two timed races. Felix and Francie's best time was 12.08 minutes. The racecourse is 80 meters long. What was their average distance per minute?

_____

29. Arnie practices sword swallowing 2.65 hours a day. What was his practice time over 8.5 days?

_____

30.   9.19
    x 0.45

31.   63.55
    x 1.07

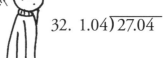

32. 1.04)27.04

33. 0.062)2.17

Name _____

PART THREE: NUMBER AND OPERATIONS—FRACTIONS

$1\frac{1}{10}$ $3\frac{1}{3}$ $\frac{5}{6}$ $3\frac{3}{9}$ $\frac{9}{15}$

$1\frac{7}{8}$ $1\frac{2}{3}$ $\frac{1}{5}$ $\frac{9}{10}$

Choose the correct fraction from the water to solve each problem.

1. $\frac{1}{2} + \frac{1}{3} =$ _____

2. $\frac{4}{10} - \frac{1}{5} =$ _____

3. $5\frac{1}{2} - 4\frac{6}{10} =$ _____

4. $\frac{12}{9} + \frac{6}{3} =$ _____

5. $5\frac{1}{4} - 3\frac{3}{8} =$ _____

6. $\frac{6}{18} + \frac{4}{3} =$ _____

Find the value of n.

7. In 3 days, Lester swam a total of $9\frac{5}{6}$ miles. He swam $3\frac{1}{2}$ miles on Monday and $4\frac{1}{3}$ miles on Tuesday. How far did he swim on Wednesday?

   $\mathbf{n} = 9\frac{5}{6} - (3\frac{1}{2} + 4\frac{1}{3})$ $\mathbf{n} = \underline{\ 2\ }$ miles

   Is the solution correct? Write **yes** or **no**. Then explain your answer.

   _____

   _____

   _____

8. When a snake snuck up behind Lucia, she swam the 40 meters to the boat in 18 seconds. She told friends that her speed was $\frac{1}{2}$ meter per second.

   Is she right? _____

   How can you tell? _____

   _____

   _____

Find the area of each figure.

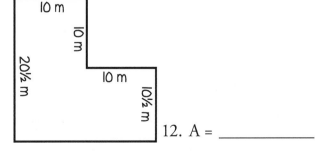

60½ m   5½ m

9. A = _____

80 ¾ ft   35 ft

10. A = _____

20¼ ft   20¼ ft

11. A = _____

10 m   10 m   20½ m   10 m   10½ m

12. A = _____

Name _____

Circle the correct answer.

13. Cici spent 3 hours a day swimming in the lake. She divided her time equally among 4 different swimming strokes. How much time did she spend on each stroke?

$\frac{4}{3}$ hr $\frac{12}{1}$ hr $\frac{12}{4}$ hr $\frac{1}{3}$ hr $\frac{3}{4}$ hr $\frac{12}{9}$ hr

14. After swim practice, 15 swimmers shared 9 sandwiches equally. How much did they each get?

$\frac{12}{9}$ $1\frac{1}{3}$ $\frac{1}{3}$ $\frac{3}{4}$ $\frac{3}{5}$ $\frac{2}{3}$ $\frac{108}{9}$

Solve the problems.

15. $\frac{6}{4} \times \frac{3}{8} =$ _____

16. $\frac{9}{16} \times \frac{1}{2} =$ _____

17. $\frac{2}{3} \times \frac{5}{7} =$ _____

18. $\frac{15}{6} \times \frac{6}{4} =$ _____

19. $1\frac{1}{2} \times \frac{3}{8} =$ _____

20. $10\frac{1}{10} \times \frac{3}{10} =$ _____

Will the product be greater than the first factor? Circle *yes* or *no*. Explain your answer.

21. $25 \times \frac{12}{15}$ yes   no

How do you know? _____

_____

_____

22. $32 \times 3\frac{1}{2}$ yes   no

How do you know? _____

_____

_____

23. $18 \times \frac{4}{3}$ yes   no

How do you know? _____

_____

_____

Use the rectangle to show a solution to each problem. Write the answer.

24. $\frac{1}{2} \div 6 =$

25. $\frac{1}{3} \times \frac{1}{4} =$

Name

PART FOUR: MEASUREMENT AND DATA

Check the accuracy of the problems. Circle *yes* or *no*. Then explain your answer.

1. Alonzo lifts 60 pounds. He says this is one-twentieth of a ton.
   Is he right?   **yes**   **no**
   How do you know? _____
   _____

2. Max's weightlifting practice began at 11:45 a.m. and ended at 2:20 p.m.
   He says it lasted $3\frac{1}{2}$ hours. Is he right?   **yes**   **no**
   How do you know? _____
   _____

3. Fans at the football game drank 140 gallons of hot chocolate.
   Lucy thinks this is over 500 quarts. Is she right?   **yes**   **no**
   How do you know? _____
   _____

4. Lucas carried the ball 75 yards during the game. He says this is 225 feet.
   Is he right?   **yes**   **no**
   How do you know? _____
   _____

Convert the measurements.

5. 4 ml = _____ l

6. 2,000 mg = _____ g

7. 6.5 m = _____ cm

8. 32 pt = _____ gal

Compare the measurements. Write >, <, 0r = in each blank.

9. 5 yd _____ 6 ft

10. 4T _____ 6 tsp

11. 20 km _____ 20,000 m

12. 2,000 kg _____ 1 metric ton

Solve the problems.

13. During the football game, the snack shop manager filled 400 cups with 80 grams of ice each. How many kilograms of ice did he use? _____

14. The snack shop sold 150 drinks. Each held 0.3 liter of soda. How many milliliters were sold? _____

15. Ted carried the ball for $12\frac{1}{2}$ minutes. Ned carried the ball for 780 seconds. Who carried the ball longest? _____

Name

Common Core Reinforcement Activities — 5th Grade Math

Basketball Game—Player Time on the Bench

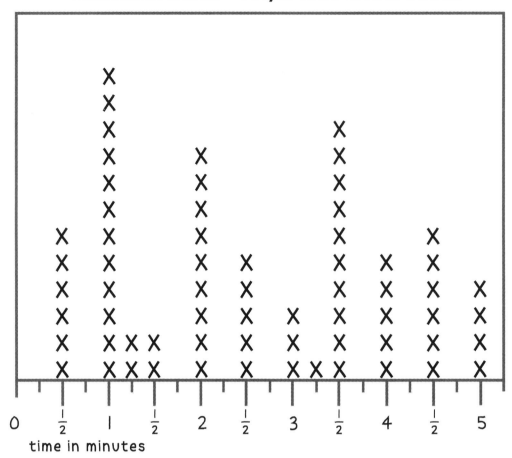

time in minutes

The basketball coach kept track of the time each player sat on the bench. Each X represents one player. Use the line plot to answer questions.

16. How many players are represented by the data? _____

17. What was the most frequent amount of time on the bench? _____

18. What is the difference between the greatest amount of time on the bench and the least amount of time on the bench? _____

19. How many players spent $1\frac{1}{4}$ minutes on the bench? _____

20. How many players spent more than $3\frac{1}{4}$ minutes on the bench? _____

Name

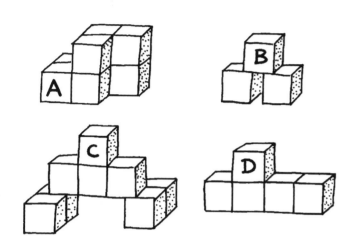

Answer the questions and follow the directions.

21. What is the volume of figure A? _____

22. If the unit is a cubic centimeter, which figure has a volume of less than 5 cm^3? _____

23. Which figure has a greater volume: A or C? _____

24. What is the volume of figure D? _____

25. Change the volume of figure B to 8 cubic units.

Solve the problems.

26. A box has measurements of 30 cm by 50 cm by 120 cm. How many decimeter cubes can be packed into the empty box? _____

27. Two boxes have the same measurements: 12 by 7 by 15 inches. What is the volume of the boxes when stacked together? _____

28. How many inch cubes can fit into an empty box with a volume of 2 cubic feet? _____

Use the figures at the right to solve the problems.

29. Which box has measurements of 2 by 3 by 2 feet? _____

30. If the width of B is 9 inches and the length is 10 inches, what is its height? _____

31. If the width of D is 5 inches and the height is 9 inches, what is its length? _____

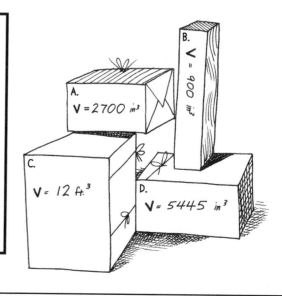

A. V = 2700 in³

B. V = 900 in³

C. V = 12 ft.³

D. V = 5445 in³

Name _____

PART FIVE: GEOMETRY

In an egg-throwing competition, eggs landed all over this grid. Use it for items 1-15.

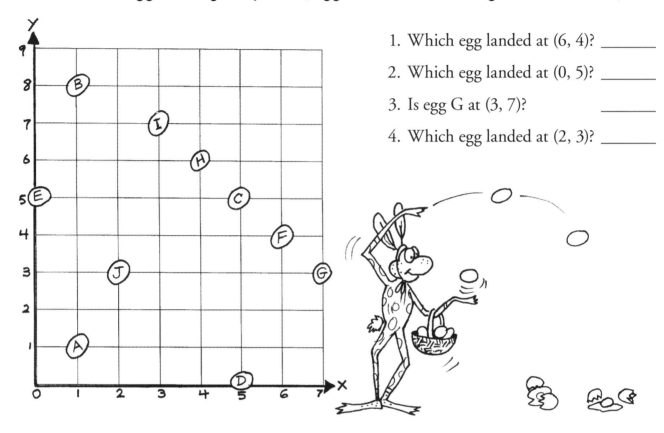

1. Which egg landed at (6, 4)? _____

2. Which egg landed at (0, 5)? _____

3. Is egg G at (3, 7)? _____

4. Which egg landed at (2, 3)? _____

Write the coordinate location for these eggs.

   5. Egg D   _____

   6. Egg A   _____

   7. Egg H   _____

   8. Egg B   _____

Draw at these locations.

   9. Draw an egg at (6, 2). Label it **K**.

  10. Draw an egg at (2, 5). Label it **L**.

Draw at these locations.

11. Draw an egg at (3, 0). Label it M.

12. Draw an egg at (6, 7). Label it N.

13. Draw an egg at (0, 7). Label it P.

14. Draw an egg at (4, 4). Label it Q.

15. A parallelogram has its corners at eggs A, J, and G. The last corner is S. Where should the last corner be located? _____ (coordinates) Draw an egg at that spot and label it **S**.

What is the length of side JG and side AS of this figure? _____

Name

Use the figures on the jump ropes for items 16–21.

16. Name figure A. _____

How many sides? _____

How many congruent sides? _____

How many congruent angles? _____

17. Which figures are parallelograms?

_____

18. Which figures have four congruent angles?

_____

19. Which figures have two or more pairs
of congruent angles?

_____

20. Which figures are trapezoids? _____

21. Which figures are rhombuses? _____

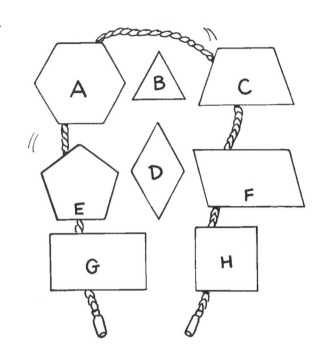

Use the flags to the right for items 22-25.

22. Which flags are scalene triangles? _____

23. Which flags are isosceles triangles? _____

24. Which flags are right triangles? _____

25. Which flags are equilateral triangles? _____

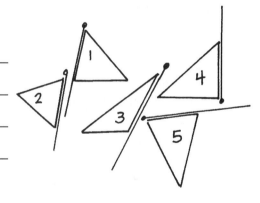

Label each statement *T* for true or *F* for false.

_____ 26. All rectangles are parallelograms.

_____ 27. A rhombus is always a rectangle.

_____ 28. A trapezoid is a parallelogram.

_____ 29. A right triangle can be isosceles.

_____ 30. Parallelograms have four right angles.

Name

ASSESSMENT ANSWER KEY

Part One: Operations and Algebraic Thinking

1. 430
2. 480
3. 21
4. 550
5. D
6. G
7. H
8. A
9. E
10. plus 10 mph
11. Each is double the
number above.
12. For each 10 mph
that the speed increases, the injuries
double.
13. 64
14. 83
15. 17
16. 50
17. 162
18. 4

Part Two: Number and Operations in Base Ten

1. taxi ride: 21,691
2. walk on stilts: 2,008
3. 70
4. 30
5. 40
6. 8×10^3
7. five
8. 450,000
9. 600
10. 6.063
11. It moves three places to the right (Answer: 8,054).
12. It moves four places to the left (Answer: 0.8024302).
13. <
14. =
15. <
16. >
17. 50,106
18. Frankie
19. Freddie
20. 18.08
21. 13.053
22. 24
23. 576
24. 4,095
25. 538,278
26. 30
27. 310, R 3
28. 0.15 m
29. 22.525 hr
30. 4.1355
31. 67.9985
32. 26
33. 35

Part Three: Number and Operations: Fractions

1. $\frac{5}{6}$
2. $\frac{1}{5}$
3. $\frac{9}{10}$
4. $3\frac{2}{9}$
5. $1\frac{7}{8}$
6. $1\frac{2}{3}$
7. yes
8. no; 18 seconds times $\frac{1}{2}$ meter would not equal 40 meters.
9. $A = 332\frac{3}{4}$ m^2
10. $A = 2,826\frac{1}{4}$ ft^2
11. $A = 410\frac{1}{16}$ ft^2
12. $A = 310$ m^2
13. $\frac{3}{4}$
14. $\frac{3}{5}$
15. $\frac{9}{16}$
16. $\frac{9}{32}$
17. $\frac{10}{21}$
18. $3\frac{3}{4}$
19. $\frac{9}{16}$
20. $3\frac{3}{100}$
21. no; the second factor is less than one, so the product will be less than the first factor.
22. yes; the second factor is greater than one, so the product will be greater than the first factor.
23. yes; the second factor is greater than one, so the product will be greater than the first factor.
24 & 25. Check diagrams to see that they present an accurate visual picture of the operation.
24. $\frac{1}{12}$
25. $\frac{1}{12}$

Part Four: Measurement and Data

1–4. Explanations will vary. Look for reasonable explanations.
1. no; A ton is 2,000 pounds. 20 times 60 is less than that.
2. no; 3 hours from 11:45 would be 2:45. $3\frac{1}{2}$ hours would be even later.
3. yes; There are 4 quarts to a gallon. 4 times 140 is over 500.
4. yes; There are 3 feet to a yard. 3 times 75 is 225.
5. 0.004 l
6. 2 g
7. 650 cm
8. 4 gal
9. >
10. >
11. =
12. >
13. 3.2
14. 45,000
15. Ned
16. 65
17. 1 minute
18. $4\frac{1}{2}$ min
19. 2
20. 25
21. 8 cubic units
22. B
23. The volume is the same.
24. 5 cubic units
25. Check drawings
to see that student has followed directions.
26. 180
27. 2,520 in^3
28. 288
29. C
30. 10 in
31. 121 in

Part Five: Geometry

1. F
2. E
3. no
4. J
5. (5, 0)
6. (1, 1)
7. (4, 6)
8. (1, 8)
9–14. Check student drawings to see that eggs are at correct
coordinate locations.
15. (6, 1); 5 units
16 hexagon; 6 sides;
6 congruent sides;
6 congruent angles
17. D, F, G, H
18. G, H
19. ALL figures
20. C
21. D, H
22. 3
23. 2, 4, 5
24. 4
25. 2
26. T
27. F
28. F
29. T
30. F

ACTIVITIES ANSWER KEY

Operations and Algebraic Thinking (pages 18–28)

Page 18

Year 1: Bathtub: 360; Bed: 41
Year 2: Bathtub: 42; Bed: 380
Year 3: Bathtub: 150; Bed: 200
Year 4: Bathtub: 57; Bed: 186
Year 5: Bathtub: 150; Bed: 440

1. 360
2. 380
3. 150
4. 186
5. 150
6. Years 3 and 5
7. no
8. Year 5
9. Year 1
10. 159

Page 19

1. Bruno, Day 2 OR Mancho, Day 1
2. Mancho, Day 2
3. Tessa, Day 1
4. Samantha, Day 2
5. Marcos, Day 1
6. Bruno, Day 1
7. Samson, Day 1
8. Samantha, Day 1

Page 20

1. Yacko: $60n + 40$
2. Yanni: $6n - 40$
3. Yang-lei: $\frac{600}{n}$
4. Yolanda: $60 - 4n$
5. Yazzi: $4(60 + n)$
6. Yuri: $\frac{60n}{2}$
7. Yvette: $6n - 4$
8. Yetty: $4n^2 - 60$
9. Yosey: $60n + 4$
10. Yanni and Yolanda

Page 21

Sunday: $9n$; $n = 45$
Monday: $n - 2$; 3
Tuesday: $n^2 + 6$; 31
Wednesday: $\frac{(n + 25)}{2}$ OR $(n + 25) \div 2$; 15
Thursday: $\frac{100}{n^2}$; 4
Friday: $2(25 - n)$; 40
Saturday: $(3(4 + n)) - 10$; 17

Page 22

1. H
2. C
3. E
4. J
5. A
6. F
7. B
8. D
9. Multiply seven times eight. Multiply four times four. Multiply the two products.
10. Multiply four times two and square the result. Add five to that.

Page 23

1. $3 \times (12 + 14)$
2. $\frac{(8 + 5 + 9)}{2}$ OR $(8 + 5 + 9) \div 2$
3. $(4 + 6) \times 6$ OR $6 \times (4 + 6)$
4. $(500 \div 50) + 45$ OR $\frac{500}{50} + 45$
5. $(30 + 90) - (8 \times 10)$

6–10: Words may vary some.

6. Subtract fifteen from the sum of fifty and thirty.
7. Subtract the sum of ten and twenty from sixteen.
8. Multiply the sum of thirteen and twelve by five.
9. half the sum of fifty-five and twenty-one
10. Add forty to the difference between twenty and eighteen.

Page 24

1. a
2. d
3. d
4. c
5. b
6. $((10 \times 4) - (20 \times 2)) \times 3$

Page 25

A. Chart: Left column blanks: 15, 18, 21, 24; Right column blanks: 5, 6, 7, 8
B. Chart: Left column blanks: 106, 107, 108; Right column blanks: 70, 65, 60

1–3 and 5–7: Descriptions may vary.

1. Add 3
2. Add 1
3. Number of snakes is 3 times the number of bites.
4. 10
5. Add one.
6. Subtract five.
7. With each additional snake over 100, the number of bites diminishes by 5.
8. 110

Pages 26–27

Completed table left column top to bottom to read: 0, 3, 6, 9, 12, 15, 18, 21, 24

Completed table right column top to bottom to read: 0, 2, 4, 6, 8, 10, 12, 14, 16

Descriptions may vary.

1. Add 3.
2. Add 2.
3. Table from top to bottom will read: (0, 0) (3, 2) (6, 4) (9, 6) (12, 8) (15, 10) (18, 12) (21, 14) (24, 16) Examine student graphs to see that the line follows the above ordered pairs.
4. Answers will vary: With each three additional chews, the diameter of the bubble increases by two inches.

Page 28

Completed table left column top to bottom to read: 50, 48, 46, 44, 42, 40, 38, 36, 34, 32

Completed table right column top to bottom to read: 50, 46, 42, 38, 34, 30, 26, 22, 18, 14

Descriptions may vary some.

1. subtract 2
2. subtract 4
3. The number of sips falls at twice the rate of decrease in the age
4. 28

Number and Operations in Base Ten (pages 30–58)

Pages 30-31

1. stuffed toy (506)
2. hamburger (21) and castle (21)
3. salami (68); paella (65)
4. scarecrow (103)
5. sausage (2889)
6. pie (40)
7. pizza (122)
8. yo-yo (10)
9. scarecrow (7 in.); paella (7 in.)
10. 80
11. 10
12. 429
13. 600
14. 30
15. 93
16. 70
17. 80
18. 200

Page 32

1. B, 267	8. A, 924
2. B, 2,424	9. B, 3,060
3. A, 6,334	10. A, 180
4. A, 518	11. A, 33
5. A, 180	12. A, 82
6. B, 49	13. B, 6,334
7. B, 56	14. B, 2,424

Page 33

1. 400,000
2. 30,000,000
3. 9×10^4
4. four (64,310,000)
5. 54×10^7
6. c
7. b
8. c

Pages 34–35

1. Decimal point moves three places to the right; 2736.1
2. Decimal point moves two places to the left; 4.1001

3. 1,224.1	12. 1,001
4. 1.954	13. 4,600
5. 6,650	14. 0.77707
6. 0.808088	15. 7,770
7. 0.02867	16. 396.6
8. 69,990	17. 5,473
9. 1,150	18. 9,000
10. 5.321	19. 0.0193105
11. 8,610	20. 1,300

Page 36

1. 70.6 hrs	5. 1,140
2. 870 mi	6. 1,746
3. 53	7. 4.026
4. 36 hr	8. 662 hr

Sand Wizards: 2,470
Sand Crabs: 3,700
Builders Four: 4.600
Sculptors: 932.66
Castle Quartet: 2,456.6

Page 37

1. $100 + (2 \times 10) + (5 \times 1) + (6 \times \frac{1}{10}) + (8 \times \frac{1}{100})$
2. $1000 + (3 \times 100) + (8 \times \frac{1}{10}) + (5 \times \frac{1}{100})$
3. $(2 \times 1000) + (2 \times 100) + (2 \times \frac{1}{10}) + (4 \times \frac{1}{100})$

4. $10 + (6 \times 1) + (5 \times \frac{1}{100}) + \frac{1}{1000}$
5. $1000 + (8 \times 1) + (5 \times \frac{1}{1000})$
6. $(5 \times 10) + (5 \times 1) + (7 \times \frac{1}{100}) + (9 \times \frac{1}{1000})$
7. 3,308.03
8. 6,020.052
9. 40,500.908

Pages 38–39

1. b	7. c
2. a	8. c
3. d	9. b
4. d	10. b
5. b	11. d
6. a	

Page 40

1. three and seventy-two hundredths
2. two and six hundred four thousandths
3. fifty-nine hundredths
4. nine and ninety-eight hundredths
5. seven and two thousandths
6. nine and nine hundredths
7. ten and fifteen thousandths
8. one and five tenths
9. eight and thirty-five hundredths
10. 12.44
11. 0.708
12. 44.22

Page 41

1. <	3. =	5. >	7. =
2. <	4. <	6. >	8. >

Pages 42–43

1. Amy	11. Roxy
2. Moe	12. Sal
3. T.J.	13. Fred
4. Thomas	14. Georgia
5. Lara	15. neither
6. Kimo	16. Lexi
7. Tex	17. neither
8. Danya	18. Lin
9. Lou	19. Charlie
10. neither	

Pages 44–45

1. 5.4	9. 39.21
2. 12.41	10. 0.6
3. 10.4	11. 3.0
4. 3.8	12. 2.69
5. 259	13. 30.1
6. 0.338	14. 2,500.1
7. 12.41	15. 78
8. 1,501	16. 75.079

Page 46

1. 56	5. 10
2. 130.3	6. 30.9
3. 63	7. 105
4. 13	8. 100

Page 47

1. Francine Frosting
2. 456 minutes (or 7 hours, 36 minutes)
3. 1,974
4. 126
5. 2,600
6. 378
7. 11,592
8. 5,742
9. 567

Pages 48-49

1. yes	7. no	13. yes
2. no	8. yes	14. no
3. no	9. no	15. yes
4. yes	10. yes	16. yes
5. no	11. no	17. yes
6. no	12. no	18. yes

Pages 50-51

1. pizza tossers
2. Year 4
3. 154
4. Year 1
5. 342
6. Year 3
7. 22-inch diameter
8. 188 pounds
9. 576
10. 572
11. 13 seconds
12. 2,994 hours

Page 52

Strategies will vary. Share strategies. Listen to them for good sense and workability.

1. 149	5. 103
2. 15	6. 804
3. 5,000	7. 153
4. 126, R10	8. 7,000

Page 53

1. 141	6. 480
2. 240	7. 286
3. 558	8. 221
4. 336	9. 231
5. 315	10. 96

Page 54

1. 7	6. 14
2. 9	7. 8
3. 12	8. 13
4. 5	9. 15
5. 6	10. 11

Page 55

Explanations will vary. Check for clarity and sense.

A. 8.02	D. 145.52
B. 12,084.6	E. 0.00608
C. 35.762	F. 0.6202

Pages 56–57

1. 11.029 ft
2. 5.08 ft
3. 126.851 ft
4. 22.24 ft
5. 21.22 ft
6. 80.7 ft
7. 35.934 ft
8. 74.425 ft
A. 30.0003
B. 18.001
C. 0.9768
D. 0.422
E. 0.006636
F. 12,000
G. 50.44
H. 24.88
I. 1.071

Page 58

Paths may vary. Path should touch some or all of the following plates:
A, D, E, F, H, J, K, L, O, P
Other wrong answers corrected:

B. 9.006	I. 90.8
C. 929.312	M. 4.9
G. 0.039	N. 10.046

Number and Operations—Fractions (pages 59–88)

Page 60

1. $\frac{5}{6}$
2. $\frac{3}{10}$
3. $\frac{1}{10}$
4. $1\frac{2}{9}$
5. $6\frac{3}{20}$
6. $\frac{16}{21}$
7. $2\frac{2}{15}$
8. $2\frac{8}{35}$
9. $12\frac{1}{12}$
10. $\frac{3}{20}$
11. $\frac{41}{63}$
12. $\frac{2}{7}$

Page 61

1. $\frac{1}{6}$
2. $\frac{13}{22}$
3. $\frac{4}{5}$
4. $\frac{1}{3}$
5. $\frac{1}{2}$
6. $\frac{19}{21}$
7. $\frac{1}{8}$
8. $\frac{1}{12}$
9. $\frac{5}{6}$
10. $\frac{3}{10}$
11. $\frac{19}{24}$
12. $\frac{1}{2}$
13. $\frac{7}{9}$
14. $\frac{4}{9}$

Page 62

Check to see that path touches these squares:

$\frac{8}{12} + \frac{2}{3}$; $\frac{20}{25} + \frac{4}{5}$;

$\frac{2}{4} - \frac{5}{10}$; $\frac{7}{12} + \frac{14}{24}$;

$\frac{6}{3} + \frac{8}{4}$; $\frac{1}{2} - \frac{2}{5}$;

$\frac{8}{4} + \frac{12}{6}$; $\frac{2}{3} - \frac{4}{6}$;

Page 63

1. $\frac{1}{6}$
2. $12\frac{1}{2}$
3. $\frac{7}{20}$
4. a; $\frac{13}{60}$
5. $\frac{3}{40}$

Page 64

Jose—no
Abby—yes
Dylan—no
Jessica—no
Ryan—no
Brad—yes
Lauren—yes
Andy—yes
Alexa—no
Denise—no
Look for well-reasoned explanations.

Page 65

1. no
2. yes
3. yes
4. no
Look for well-reasoned explanations.

Page 66

1. c
2. c
3. b
4. a
5. a
6. b

Page 67

Look for reasonable explanations that show understanding of a fraction as division.

1. Correct; $\frac{16}{30}$ represents the need to divide the time of 16 meters by 30 seconds. $\frac{16}{30}$ minutes times the 30 meters she swam = 16.

2. Incorrect; the three chests must be divided among five divers. Each diver would get $\frac{3}{5}$ of a chest because $\frac{3}{5}$ times 5 = 3.

3. Correct; $\frac{99}{6}$ shows the amount of money divided by the number of dives. $\frac{\$99}{6}$ per dive times 6 dives equals $99.

4. Incorrect; the 9 fish must be divided among 12 divers. The fraction $\frac{9}{12}$ accurately represents this division because $\frac{9}{12}$ fish each times the 12 divers results in 9 whole fish.

Page 68

Sunday: $\frac{6}{8}$ lb

Monday: $\frac{9}{7}$ hr

Tuesday: $\frac{12}{15}$ liters

Wednesday: $\frac{\$40}{6}$

Thursday: $\frac{7}{15}$ hr

Friday: $\frac{50}{16}$ lb

Saturday: $\frac{10}{14}$ bowl

Page 69

1. d
2. a
3. b
4. c
5. b
6. c

Page 70

1. $\frac{32}{9}$ or $3\frac{5}{9}$ hr
2. $\frac{27}{3}$ or 9 m
3. $\frac{50}{9}$ or $5\frac{5}{9}$ hr
4. $\frac{8}{3}$ or $2\frac{2}{3}$ yd
5. $\frac{7}{3}$ or $2\frac{1}{3}$ hr
6. $\frac{36}{5}$ or $7\frac{1}{5}$ m
7. $\frac{45}{3}$ or 15
8. $\frac{15}{2}$ or $7\frac{1}{2}$
9. $\frac{ad}{b}$
10. $\frac{96}{16}$ or 6
11. $\frac{10}{11}$
12. $\frac{72}{4}$ or 18 lb

Page 71

1. $\frac{ag}{d}$
2. $\frac{30}{6}$
3. $\frac{3}{8}$
4. $\frac{10}{28}$
5. $\frac{10}{80}$
6. $\frac{ab}{g}$
7. $\frac{14}{27}$
8. $\frac{9}{20}$
9. $\frac{28}{10}$
10. $\frac{24}{30}$
11. $\frac{48}{40}$
12. $\frac{30}{24}$

Pages 72–73

A. $332\frac{3}{4}$ m^2
B. $2,826\frac{1}{4}$ ft^2
C. $410\frac{1}{16}$ ft^2
D. $240\frac{1}{4}$ ft^2
E. $21,070$ m^2
F. 310 m^2
G. $1,508\frac{1}{125}$ m^2
H. $8,811$ yd^2
I. $350\frac{1}{2}$ m^2

Page 74

1. $\frac{1}{8}$ hr
2. $\frac{3}{8}$ of the team
3. $7\frac{1}{5}$ lb
4. $\frac{14}{36}$ (or $\frac{7}{18}$)
   Note: Use $\frac{7}{12} \times \frac{2}{3}$ because the question asks what fraction of the set was in good shape—not what fraction was broken.)
5. $\frac{64}{10}$ or $6\frac{2}{5}$ mi
6. 135 lb
7. 27 ft
8. 35

Page 75

1. The area of Lucas' strip will be half the area of the regular strip because the length is being multiplied by half of the amount.

2. The product of 150 x 150 will be 6 times the product of 150 x 25 because the factor 150 is six times the size of the factor 25.

3. No. $\frac{5}{6}$ is greater than $\frac{3}{4}$ so the product of $\frac{5}{6}$ x 12 will be greater than $\frac{3}{4}$ x 12.

4. Shura's bout will be $\frac{1}{10}$ x 9 longer because $\frac{3}{5}$ is $\frac{1}{10}$ greater than $\frac{1}{2}$.

5. Yes. The factor 12 is $\frac{3}{4}$ of the factor 16.

6. The product of 60 x 88 will be $1\frac{1}{2}$ times the product of 88 x 40 because the factor 60 is $1\frac{1}{2}$ times the size of the factor 40.

Page 76

1. No. $\frac{9}{10}$ less than one, so the product will be less than 15.

2. Yes. $\frac{9}{8}$ is greater than one, so the product will be greater than 100.

3. Yes. $3\frac{1}{2}$ is greater than one, so the product will be greater than 65.

4. Yes. $\frac{6}{4}$ is greater than one, so the product will be greater than 21.

5. No. $\frac{7}{9}$ is less than one, so the product will be less than 33.

6. No. $\frac{3}{4}$ is less than one, so the product will be less than 175.

7. Yes. $2\frac{3}{4}$ is greater than one, so the product will be greater than 72.

8. Yes. $\frac{9}{7}$ is greater than one, so the product will be greater than 49.

Page 77

1. <; $\frac{5}{6}$ is less than one, so $\frac{5}{6}$ times any other factor will result in a product less than that factor.

2. =; multiplying by $\frac{7}{7}$ is the same as multiplying by 1. The product will be $\frac{6}{8}$—the same as the factor.

3. >; $\frac{8}{6}$ is greater than one, so $\frac{8}{6}$ times any other factor will result in a product greater than that factor.

4. >; $3\frac{2}{5}$ is greater than one, so $3\frac{2}{5}$ times any other factor will result in a product greater than that factor.

5. <; $\frac{7}{8}$ is less than one, so $\frac{7}{8}$ times any other factor will result in a product less than that factor.

6. Between 21 and 24; 7×3 is 21 so $7\frac{1}{2} \times 3$ will be greater than 21. But $7\frac{1}{2}$ is less than 8. 8×3 would be 24.

7. Between 48 and 72. 2×24 is 48 so $2\frac{2}{3}$ will be greater than 48. But $2\frac{2}{3}$ is less than 3, so the product will not be as great as 72—which is 3×24.

Page 78

1. $2\frac{1}{2} \times \frac{3}{4} = \frac{15}{8}$ or $1\frac{7}{8}$ t

2. $4 \times \frac{2}{3} = \frac{8}{3}$ or $2\frac{2}{3}$ C

3. $2 \times 3\frac{1}{4} = 6\frac{1}{2}$

4. $\frac{1}{5} \times 3\frac{1}{2} = \frac{7}{10}$ C

5. $\frac{1}{2} \times 3\frac{1}{4} = 1\frac{5}{8}$ bananas

6. $3 \times 3\frac{1}{2} = \frac{21}{2} = 10\frac{1}{2}$ C

Page 79

Equations may vary. Check to see that equations represent problems accurately.

1. $\frac{2}{3} \times \frac{4}{5} = n$;
(n = $\frac{8}{15}$ hour)
$\frac{8}{15} \times 60 = n$;
(n = $\frac{480}{15}$ = 32 minutes)

2. $\frac{1}{4} \times 8\frac{3}{9} = n$;
(n = $2\frac{3}{36}$ OR $2\frac{1}{12}$);
$8\frac{3}{9} - 2\frac{1}{12} = n$;
(n = $6\frac{9}{36}$ OR $6\frac{1}{4}$ ounces)

3. $5 \times \frac{1}{2} = n$; (n = $\frac{5}{2}$);
$8 + \frac{5}{2} = n$; (n = $10\frac{1}{2}$);
$10\frac{1}{2} \times 6\frac{1}{2} = n$;
(n = $\frac{273}{4}$ OR $68\frac{1}{4}$
OR $68.25)

4. $\frac{3}{4} \times \frac{4}{12} = n$; (n = $\frac{12}{48}$
OR $\frac{1}{4}$ hour);
$\frac{1}{4} \times 60 = n$ (n = $\frac{60}{4}$
OR 15 minutes)

5. $\frac{1}{4} \times \frac{4}{9} = n$;
(n = $\frac{4}{36}$ = $\frac{1}{9}$)

6. $\frac{2}{7} \times 15\frac{3}{4} = n$;
(n = $\frac{126}{32}$ OR
$3\frac{15}{16}$ pounds)

Page 80

$13\frac{3}{4}$ lb potatoes

$20\frac{5}{8}$ quarts boiling water

5 large onions

$20\frac{5}{16}$ cups chicken broth

$11\frac{2}{3}$ carrots

$21\frac{1}{4}$ celery sticks

$3\frac{3}{4}$ green peppers

$13\frac{1}{3}$ cups frozen corn

$11\frac{1}{4}$ pounds mushrooms

$18\frac{1}{8}$ cups cooked chicken

$5\frac{5}{6}$ teaspoons salt

$15\frac{5}{6}$ Tablespoons mixed herbs

Page 81

1. 15 pounds

2. $3\frac{1}{6}$ minutes (OR 3 minutes, 10 seconds)

3. 68 ounces

4. 40 min

Page 82

Examine student models to see that they show the problem accurately.

1. $\frac{1}{10}$ 5. $\frac{1}{12}$

2. $\frac{3}{14}$ 6. $\frac{3}{16}$

3. $\frac{2}{12}$ 7. $\frac{1}{6}$

4. $\frac{4}{15}$ 8. $\frac{4}{20}$

Page 83

1. b   4. a

2. a   5. c

3. b   6. c

Page 84

Explanations will vary. Check to see that explanation shows understanding of the division process and supports a correct

answer.

1. yes

2. no

3. no

4. yes

5. no

6. no

7. $5 \div \frac{1}{4}$

Page 85

Explanations will vary. Check to see that explanation shows understanding of the division process and supports a correct answer.

1. 4 million

2. 160

3. 50

4. 5

5. 45

Pages 86–87

Explanations will vary. Check to see that explanation shows understanding of the division process and supports a correct answer.

1. yes

2. yes

3. no

4. no

5. no

6. yes

7. no

8. yes

Page 88

Examine models for accurate answer and demonstration that student understands the concepts of dividing a fraction by a whole number and a whole number by a fraction.

1. 6

2. $\frac{3}{25}$

3. 8

4. $\frac{2}{9}$

5. $\frac{2}{12}$ or $\frac{1}{6}$

Measurement and Data (Pages 90–106)

Page 90

1. no
2. no
3. yes
4. no
5. no
6. yes
7. no
8. yes
9. yes
10. both

Page 91

1. >
2. =
3. >
4. =
5. =
6. >
7. =
8. =
9. <
10. <
11. <
12. =
13. <
14. <
15. <
16. >
17. >
18. <
19. =
20. >

Page 92

1. Any of these: inches, feet, yards, miles, millimeters, centimeters, decimeters, meters, kilometers
2. correct
3. correct
4. correct
5. 2 kilometers
6. 100
7. 1,000
8. correct
9. correct
10. 5,000
11. correct
12. correct
13. correct
14. correct
15. 10,000
16. 10
   Yes, Ted will pass the test.

Page 93

1. 1,080 cups
2. 2 gal
3. 96
4. 1.5 kg
5. 9
6. $429
7. $2\frac{1}{2}$ hr
8. 300 km

Page 94

Check line plots for correct number of X's

$\frac{1}{2}$ 2		4	0
1 2		$4\frac{1}{4}$	1
$1\frac{1}{2}$ 1		$4\frac{1}{2}$	3
2 3		5	1
$2\frac{1}{2}$ 4		$5\frac{1}{2}$	6
3 2		6	1
$3\frac{1}{2}$ 1			

Page 95

1. 4 (Note: Question asks about fifths, not tenths—use equivalent fraction.)
2. 20 (Note: Question asks about fifths, not tenths—use equivalent fraction.)
3. 9 (Note: Translate fraction of minutes to seconds.)
4. 24
5. 65
6. $\frac{1}{10}$ and $\frac{2}{10}$
7. Answers may vary. Most of the bubbles lasted $\frac{3}{10}$ to $\frac{7}{10}$ of a minute.

Page 96

1. 44
2. $\frac{13}{16}$
3. 19
4. 3
5. 2
6. 4

Page 97

Check line plots for correct numbers of X's:

$\frac{1}{10}$	—	1
$\frac{1}{5}$	—	1
$\frac{3}{10}$	—	1
$\frac{5}{10}$	—	2
$\frac{4}{5}$	—	5
$1\frac{1}{10}$	—	4
$1\frac{1}{5}$	—	6
$1\frac{3}{5}$	—	3
$1\frac{7}{10}$	—	2
$1\frac{9}{10}$	—	1

Page 98

1. 18
2. $4\frac{3}{4}$ inches
3. (3) $32\frac{3}{4}$ & 34
   (4) $31\frac{1}{2}$ & 35;
   (5) $32\frac{1}{2}$ & 34;
   (6) $31\frac{1}{2}$ & $34\frac{1}{2}$;
   (8) $30\frac{1}{4}$ & $34\frac{3}{4}$;
   (9) 32 & $33\frac{3}{4}$
   (10) $32\frac{1}{4}$ & $33\frac{1}{2}$;
   (12) 31 & $31\frac{3}{4}$ & $34\frac{1}{4}$
4. 18
5. 26
6. 134

page 99

1. 21
2. 14
3. (1) $2\frac{9}{10}$ & $2\frac{19}{20}$
   (3) $2\frac{1}{20}$ & $2\frac{7}{20}$ & $2\frac{9}{20}$;
   (5) $2\frac{5}{20}$ & $2\frac{11}{20}$ & $2\frac{15}{20}$ & $2\frac{8}{10}$;
   (7) $2\frac{2}{10}$ & $2\frac{4}{10}$;
   (12) $2\frac{3}{10}$ & $2\frac{17}{20}$
4. 3
5. $2\frac{3}{20}$ kg
6. 110

Pages 100–101

1. E
2. J
3. 5 cubic units
4. B
5. 12
6. no
7. G and I
8. 4 cubic units
9. three: F, G, I
10. five: B, C, D, H, K
11. 40
12. Check student drawing to see that the structure has a volume of 31 cubic units.

Page 102

1. $1\frac{1}{2}$ ft^3
2. 343 in^3
3. 15 in
4. 0.6 m^3
5. 80 cm
6. no

Page 103

1. 1,500 cm^3
2. 2,250 cm^3
3. 2,500 cm^3
4. 4,000 cm^3
5. 1,500 cm^3
6. 3,750 cm^3
7. 1,344 cm^3
A. Maria and Val
B. Sal

Pages 104–105

1. D
2. E
3. H
4. C
5. B
6. A
7. F
8. G

The hockey uniforms need the biggest box.

Page 106

Measurements will vary. Check to see that measurement by counting cubes agrees with measurement and formula calculation.

Geometry (pages 108–126)

Page 108

1. (-2, 2); (2, 8); (4, 9)
2. (-4, 4); (7, 8)
3. (-3, 8); (4, 3)
4. (-6, 9); (6, 5)
5. (-5, 6); (6, 3)
6. (-4, 0); (-6, 2); (7, 1)

Page 109

Check grid to see that objects are drawn at specified locations.

Page 110

A. (-6, 5)
B. (-2, 2)
C. (3, 4)
D. (-6, -2)
E. (-4, 4)
F. (4, -2)
G. (-4, -6)
H. (3, -5)
I. (5, 3)
J. (6, 1)
K. (-5, -4)
L. (1, -6)
M. (-2, -6)
N. (-2, 5)
O. (1, 3)
P. (5, -3)
Q. (4, 0)

Page 111

Check grid to see that points are plotted at specified locations to create an image of a snail.

Pages 112-113

Check grid to see that points are plotted at specified locations.

#3. Climbers' paths touch or cross at 3 places: (-3, 0); (approx 3.5, 3.5); (approx -1.5, 6.5)

Page 114

1. yes
2. (8, 9)
3. (10, 2)
4. -18

Check grid to see that points are plotted at specified locations.

Page 115

Check grid to see that points are plotted at specified locations.

Page 116

1. yes
2. yes
3. no
4. no
5. no
6. yes
7. yes
8. no
9. yes
10. (10, 2)

Check grid to see that points are plotted at specified locations.

Page 117

1–7: Check grid to see that points are plotted at specified locations.
8–11: Check to see that coordinates match student drawings.

Page 118

1. 6
2. 21
3. 10
4. 81
5. 123

Page 119

1. She added 10 new tattoos in year 8.
2. plus 6
3. 69
4. She added 7 new tattoos in year 4.
5. no year
6. (2, 10) and (3, 4)
7. (4, 7) and (5, 7) OR (7, 10) and (8, 10)
8. 89

Page 120

1. (6, 9)
2. (11, 3)
3. (6, 5)
4. (8, 1) OR (12, 5)

Check to see that figures are drawn accurately and that all missing corners are labeled.

Page 121

1. E
2. C or I
3. A, I, or L
4. D
5. I
6. E
7. B
8. F
9. E
10. K

Page 122

A. octagon
B. hexagon
C. pentagon
D. trapezoid
E. square
F. rectangle
G. parallelogram, square, rectangle
H. quadrilateral
I. obtuse triangle
J. equilateral triangle
K. right triangle
L. scalene triangle
M. triangle
N. polygon
O. isosceles
P. rhombus (or square)

Page 123

Answers may vary. Check them for accuracy.

1. SPQ or SQT; An equilateral triangle has congruent (equal) sides and angles.
2. QTR or TRU; An isosceles triangle has at least two congruent (equal) sides and angles.
3. QNO or ONU; A scalene triangle has no congruent (equal) sides or angles.
4. PMQ or PMS; A right triangle is a triangle with one right angle.
5. parallelogram; It has two pairs of parallel sides.
6. trapezoid; It has one pair of parallel sides and one pair of nonparallel sides.
7. a pentagon; It has five sides.

Page 124

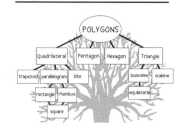

Page 125

1. A parallelogram has two PAIRS of parallel sides, not just 2 parallel sides.
2. A trapezoid could be a right trapezoid with one right angle.
3. For a right triangle to be equilateral, all three angles would have to be 90° each. This would give an angle sum of 270°, but the sum of all angles in any triangle is 180°.
4. A rhombus can have 4 right angles, but a figure can have 4 equal sides without 4 right angles.
5. The sum of angles in a triangle is 180°; 80 + 80 + 60 (220) is greater than 180.
6. The definition of a rectangle does not include four equal sides. A figure can be a rectangle without being a square.
7. To be a regular pentagon, all sides and angles must be congruent. If angles are not congruent, the sides could not be equal.
8. The sum of angles in any quadrilateral is 360°.

Page 126

Check drawings to see that they match descriptions and names.

A. isosceles triangle
B. rectangle
C. scalene triangle
D. right trapezoid
E. parallelogram
F. rhombus (or parallelogram)